lonely planet

BEST ROAD TRIPS
CANADIAN
ROCKIES

- - - - - - - →

ESCAPES ON THE OPEN ROAD

Ray Bartlett, Gregor Clark, John Lee,
Craig McLachlan, Brendan Sainsbury

SYMBOLS IN THIS BOOK

✓ Top Tips	History & Culture	Essential Photo
S Link Your Trips	Family	🏃 Walking Tour
Tips from Locals	Food & Drink	✕ Eating
Trip Detour	Outdoors	🛏 Sleeping

✆ Telephone Number	@ Internet Access	English-Language Menu
⊘ Opening Hours	🛜 Wi-Fi Access	Family-Friendly
P Parking	Vegetarian Selection	Pet-Friendly
Nonsmoking	Swimming Pool	
Air-Conditioning		

MAP LEGEND

Routes
Trip Route
Trip Detour
Linked Trip
Walk Route
Tollway
Freeway
Primary
Secondary
Tertiary
Lane
Unsealed Road
Plaza/Mall
Steps
Tunnel
Pedestrian Overpass
Walk Track/Path

Boundaries
International
State/Province
Cliff

Hydrography
River/Creek
Swamp/Mangrove
Canal
Water
Dry/Salt/ Intermittent Lake
Glacier

Route Markers
Trans-Canada Hwy
Provincial/ Territorial Hwy
US National Hwy
US Interstate Hwy
US State Hwy

Trips
1 Trip Numbers
9 Trip Stop
Walking tour
Trip Detour

Population
❂ Capital (National)
◉ Capital (State/Province)
● City/Large Town
● Town/Village

Areas
Beach
Cemetery (Christian)
Cemetery (Other)
Park
Forest Reservation
Urban Area
Sportsground

Transport
Airport
Cable Car/ Funicular
Metro/Muni station
Parking
Subway station
Train/Railway
Tram

Note: Not all symbols displayed above appear on the maps in this book

CONTENTS

ROAD TRIP ESSENTIALS

TERRITORY ACKNOWLEDGEMENT

Lonely Planet would like to acknowledge and pay respect to the Indigenous people throughout this country. This guide was written on and is written about land which includes their traditional lands, unceded territories and Treaty territories. We also recognise the ongoing efforts of Indigenous peoples for reconciliation, justice, and social, cultural, and economic self-determination. We hope you can use the opportunity of your travels to connect with the people and learn about Indigenous culture and society.

COVID-19

We have re-checked every business in this book before publication to ensure that it is still open after the COVID-19 outbreak. However, the economic and social impacts of COVID-19 will continue to be felt long after the outbreak has been contained, and many businesses, services and events referenced in this guide may experience ongoing restrictions. Some businesses may be temporarily closed, have changed their opening hours and services, or require bookings; some unfortunately could have closed permanently. We suggest you check with venues before visiting for the latest information.

WELCOME TO THE
CANADIAN ROCKIES

Journey through some of North America's most spectacular landscapes, with emerald-hued glacial lakes and snowy peaks, thick forest and white-water rivers.

Whether you're keen to dip in a hot spring, hike to a 515-million-year-old fossil or savour fresh-roasted coffee in a vibrant town, the three trips in this book will take you there.

Get your culture and history fix at a local museum, or stretch your legs with a walking-tour in Vancouver or Calgary. Cycle down the longest cycling descent in Canada, or relax in a riverside log chalet – over the following pages, the choice is yours.

And we haven't even mentioned the jaw-dropping wildlife viewing yet. Catch a glimpse of bighorn sheep, local elk, bears, marmots and plenty of moose as you traverse the region's most scenic national parks, from Jasper and Banff to Kootenay and Yoho.

Time to hit the road.

Moraine Lake
RAFAEL CLASSEN/500PX ©

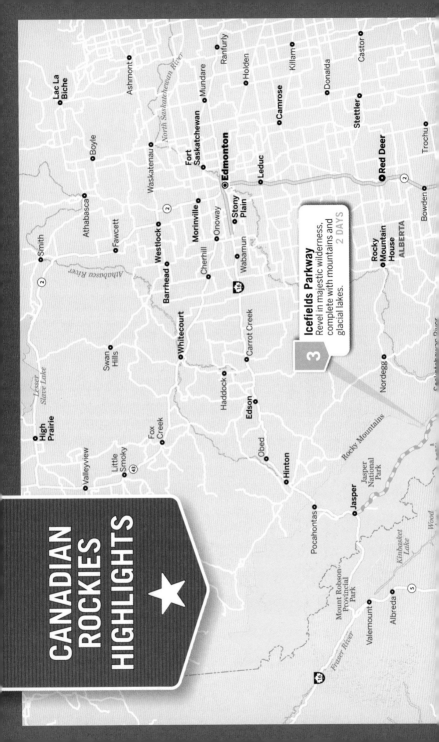

CANADIAN ROCKIES HIGHLIGHTS

3 Icefields Parkway
Revel in majestic wilderness, complete with mountains and glacial lakes.
2 DAYS

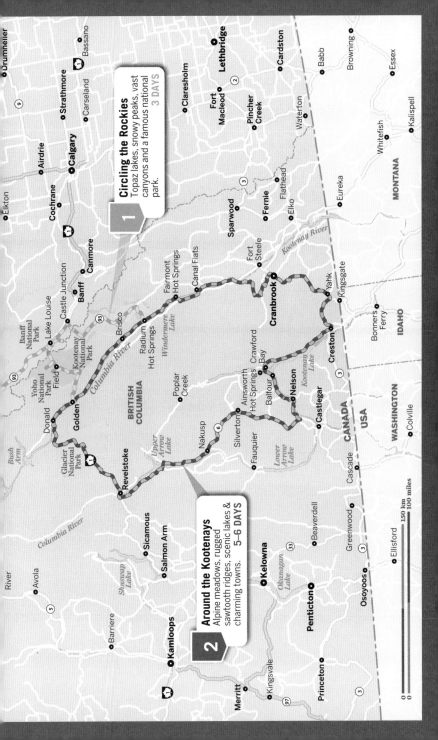

Circling the Rockies
Topaz lakes, snowy peaks, vast canyons and a famous national park.

1 **3 DAYS**

Around the Kootenays
Alpine meadows, rugged sawtooth ridges, scenic lakes & charming towns.

2 **5–6 DAYS**

Drumheller

Bassano

Strathmore

Carseland

Airdrie

Calgary

Cochrane

Claresholm

Lethbridge

Cardston

Babb

Browning

Essex

Elkton

Castle Junction

Canmore

Banff

Fort Macleod

Pincher Creek

Waterton

Kalispell

Whitefish

Lake Louise

Banff National Park

Fairmont Hot Springs

Canal Flats

Sparwood

Fernie

Flathead

Elko

Eureka

MONTANA

Field

Kootenay National Park

Yoho National Park

Brisco

Radium Hot Springs

Windermere Lake

Fort Steele

Cranbrook

Yahk

Kingsgate

Bonners Ferry

IDAHO

Donald

Golden

Columbia River

Poplar Creek

Crawford Bay

Creston

Glacier National Park

Revelstoke

Bush Arm

BRITISH COLUMBIA

Nakusp

Ainsworth Hot Springs

Balfour

Nelson

Castlegar

Kootenay Lake

Colville

WASHINGTON

CANADA

USA

Cascade

Sicamous

Salmon Arm

Columbia River

Shuswap Lake

Upper Arrow Lake

Silverton

Fauquier

Lower Arrow Lake

Greenwood

Beaverdell

Ellisford

River

Avola

Barriere

Kamloops

Kelowna

Okanagan Lake

Penticton

Osoyoos

Merritt

Kingsvale

Princeton

150 km
100 miles

0
0

CANADIAN ROCKIES
HIGHLIGHTS
★

Lake Louise (left) Ringed by an impressive amphitheater of mountains, the robin-egg-blue waters of Lake Louise are a sight to behold. See it on Trips **1** and **3**

Peyto Lake (above) Take in the lake's otherworldly emerald waters, then hike on to Bow Summit Lookout for breathtaking views and scurrying marmots. See it on Trip **3**

Golden Base yourself here for winter ski adventures and summer mountain biking at Kicking Horse Mountain Resort (right). See it on Trip **2**

CITY GUIDE

View from Stanley Park, toward Coal Harbour

VANCOUVER

Vancouver always lands atop the 'best places to live' lists, and who's to argue? Sea-to-sky beauty surrounds the laid-back, cocktail-lovin' metropolis. With skiable mountains on the outskirts, beaches fringing the core and Stanley Park's thick rainforest just blocks from downtown's glass skyscrapers, it's a harmonic convergence of city and nature.

Getting Around

Transit in Vancouver is cheap, extensive and generally efficient. Vancouver's TransLink (www.translink.ca) bus network is extensive. The SkyTrain system is fast but limited to only a few routes.

Parking

There are some free spots on residential side streets but many require permits. Numerous streets have metered parking (up to $6 per hour). Pay-parking lots (typically from $6 per hour) are a better proposition – arrive before 9am at some for early-bird, day-rate discounts. For a map of parking-lot locations, check EasyPark (www.easypark.ca).

Where to Eat

Vancouver has an eye-popping array of generally good-value dine-out options. Gastown has innovative independent dining rooms, while Main Street offers quirky indie restaurants and neighborhood hangouts. Chinatown, not surprisingly, has some top-notch authentic eateries.

Where to Stay

Staying in downtown puts you within walking distance to stores, restaurants, nightlife and some attractions. The West End is near Stanley Park with many midrange restaurants nearby.

Useful Websites

Scout Magazine (www.scoutmagazine.ca) Hip food and bar scene zine.

Tourism Vancouver (www.tourismvancouver.com) Official tourism site.

Lonely Planet (www.lonelyplanet.com/canada/vancouver) Destination information and reviews.

Cafe on Stephen Avenue Walk

CALGARY

Calgary is an urban landscape tempered by the gentle Bow River, which runs right through the core of downtown. This area boasts a multitude of inner-city neighbourhoods with an attractive jumble of bars and cafes that are as inviting on a crisp January weekend as they are on a hot afternoon in June.

Getting Around

Calgary Transit (www.calgarytransit.com) is efficient and clean. Use the website's handy plan-your-trip section to find out how to get where you're going. You can choose from the Light Rapid Transit (LRT) rail system, aka the C-Train, and ordinary buses.

Parking

Parking in downtown Calgary is an expensive nightmare – a policy designed to push people to use public transportation. Luckily, downtown hotels generally have garages. Private lots charge about $20 per day. There is also some metered parking, which accepts coins and credit cards. Outside the downtown core, parking is free and easy to find.

Where to Eat

In Calgary, the restaurant scene is blossoming, with lots of options for great eats in all price ranges. Where solitary cows once roamed, vegetables and herbs now prosper, meaning that trusty old stalwart, Alberta beef, is no longer the only thing on the menu.

You'll find good eat streets in Kensington, Inglewood, Uptown 17th Ave and downtown on Stephen Ave.

Where to Stay

Downtown is pricey, although many hotels run frequent specials. Business-oriented hotels are often cheaper over weekends. Near the city's western edge (near the Banff Trail C-Train station), you'll find every chain hotel you can think of.

Useful Websites

Visit Calgary (www.visitcalgary.com)

Alpine Club of Canada (www.acccalgary.ca) The Calgary section organizes hiking and skiing expeditions from the Bow Valley to Kananaskis.

NEED ᵀᴼ KNOW

CURRENCY
Canadian dollar ($)

LANGUAGES
English

VISAS
Visitors may require a visa to enter Canada. Those exempt require an Electronic Travel Authorization (eTA; $7), with the exception of Americans. See www.cic.gc.ca/english/visit/eta-start.asp.

FUEL
Gas is sold in liters on major highways. Expect to pay around $1.30 to $1.50 per liter, with higher prices in more remote areas. Alberta is cheaper than BC, often by around 30¢ a liter.

RENTAL CARS
Be sure to have an international license if you're not from an English- or French-speaking country.

Avis (www.avix.ca)
Budget (www.budget.com)
Hertz (www.hertz.com)
Zipcar (www.zipcar.ca)

IMPORTANT NUMBERS
Emergency (☏ 911)
Ambulance, police, fire, mountain rescue.

Roadside assistance
(☏ 1 800-222-4357)

Climate

- Dry climate
- Warm to hot summers, mild winters
- Summers – mild to warm (north & east) & warm to hot (south), cold winters
- Polar climate

Churchill GO Sep–Nov
Banff GO Jul–Sep
Vancouver GO Jun–Aug
Montréal GO Jun–Aug
Halifax GO Jul–Sep

When to Go

High Season (Jun-Aug)
» Sunshine and warm weather prevail throughout the region.

» Accommodations prices reach a peak, sometimes 50% above low season.

» Festivals and farmers markets abound in communities large and small.

Shoulder (Apr & May, Sep & Oct)
» Temperatures are cool but comfortable; rain is typical.

» Crowds and accommodations prices reduced.

» Hours for attractions outside cities are often reduced.

Low Season (Nov–Mar)
» Snow and cold (below freezing) temperatures, especially in the north.

» The year's best hotel rates, except in ski resorts.

» Outside resorts and cities, visitor attractions may be closed.

Daily Costs

Budget: Less than $100

» Dorm bed: $30–45

» Campsite: $25–40

» Food court or street-food-vendor lunch: $8–10

» Transit day pass: $5–10

Midrange: $100–300

» En suite standard hotel room: $150–200

» Meal in midrange local restaurant (excluding drinks): $15–25

» Admission to top local attraction: $15–30

» Two drinks in local pub: $15–20

Top End: More than $300

» Boutique hotel or posh B&B: $250

» Three-course meal in good restaurant (excluding drinks): $75

» Car hire: up to $75 per day

» Ski day pass: $60–100

Eating

Restaurants A full menu of options, from mom-and-pop operations to high-end spots for special occasions.

Cafes From sandwich-serving coffee shops to chatty local haunts, cafes are common and usually good value.

Bars Most bars also serve food, typically of the pub-grub variety.

Food trucks Vancouver is the food-truck capital and you'll find pockets of wheeled wonders elsewhere throughout the region.

Farmers markets Ubiquitous in summer; a great way to sample regional produce and local-made treats.

The following price ranges refer to a main course.

$ less than $15

$$ $15–25

$$$ more than $25

Sleeping

Hotels Choices range from modest motels to deluxe resorts.

B&Bs Often in the higher price bracket, but midrange options are common away from the big cities.

Campgrounds & Hostels Book as soon as possible for campsites in top areas, as they often sell out fast. Private rooms in hostels are highly sought-after in summer.

The price ranges below are for a double room in high season, before taxes and tips.

$ less than $100

$$ $100–250

$$$ more than $250

Arriving in the Canadian Rockies

Vancouver International Airport SkyTrain's Canada Line runs to the city center ($9.20) every few minutes from 5:10am to 12:57am. Travel time around 25 minutes. Taxis to city-center hotels cost $35 to $45 (30 minutes).

Calgary International Airport Allied Airport Shuttles runs shuttle buses every 30 minutes from 8am to midnight ($15). Downtown-bound taxis cost around $40 (30 minutes).

Edmonton International Airport Sky Shuttle airport buses run to city hotels ($18), taking about 45 minutes to reach downtown. Taxis from the airport cost about $50.

Internet Access

Free wi-fi connections are almost standard in accommodations across BC and Alberta. You'll find wi-fi and internet-access computers in libraries, and free wi-fi in coffee shops and other businesses.

Money

ATMs widely available. Credit cards accepted in most hotels and restaurants.

Tipping

Tipping is expected in Canada. Typical rates:

Bar servers $1 per drink

Hotel bellhops $1 to $2 per bag for bellhops.

Hotel cleaners $2 per day

Restaurant wait staff 15%

Taxi drivers 10% to 15%

Opening Hours

Banks 9am or 10am–5pm Monday to Friday; some open 9am to noon Saturday

Bars 11am–midnight or later; some only open from 5pm

Restaurants breakfast 7am–11am, lunch 11:30am–2pm, dinner 5pm–9:30pm (8pm in rural areas)

Shops 10am–5pm or 6pm Monday to Saturday, noon–5pm Sunday; some (especially in malls) open to 8pm or 9pm Thursday and/or Friday

Supermarkets 9am–8pm; some open 24 hours

For more, see Road Trip Essentials (p109).

Road Trips

Icefields Parkway
BENEDEK/GETTY IMAGES ©

Circling the Rockies

Taking you through Kootenay, Banff and Yoho National Parks and dipping into Alberta, this trip shows off nature at its best – lofty snow-capped mountains, deep forests and natural hot springs.

TRIP HIGHLIGHTS

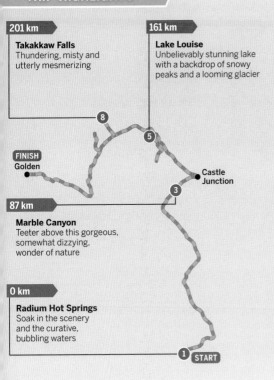

201 km

Takakkaw Falls
Thundering, misty and utterly mesmerizing

161 km

Lake Louise
Unbelievably stunning lake with a backdrop of snowy peaks and a looming glacier

FINISH
Golden

Castle Junction

87 km

Marble Canyon
Teeter above this gorgeous, somewhat dizzying, wonder of nature

0 km

Radium Hot Springs
Soak in the scenery and the curative, bubbling waters

1 START

**3 DAYS
294KM/183 MILES**

GREAT FOR...

BEST TIME TO GO
July and August when the snow has melted and all of the roads are open

ESSENTIAL PHOTO
Mt Temple Viewpoint in Banff National Park for postcard-perfect mountain shots

BEST FOR WILDLIFE
Watch for bears, elk, bighorn sheep and plenty of moose

ootenay National Park Bighorn sheep

1 Circling the Rockies

This route will give you a new perspective on nature. This is where mountains stretch up to the stars and where bears and moose own the woods (and sometimes the road). Waterfalls, canyons and gem-colored lakes lay deep in the forest, waiting to be discovered. It's impossible not to be awed, not to feel small, and not to wish you had longer to explore.

❶ Radium Hot Springs (p70)

Set in a valley just inside the southern border of **Kootenay National Park**, the outdoor **Radium Hot Springs** (☎250-347-9485; www.pc.gc.ca/hotsprings; off Hwy 93; adult/child $7.30/4.95; ⏰9am-11pm) has a hot pool simmering at 102°F (39°C) and a second pool to cool you off at 84°F (29°C). Originally sacred to indigenous groups for the water's curative powers, these springs are uniquely odorless and colorless. The large tiled

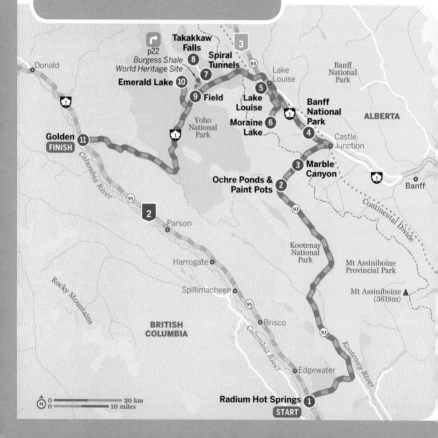

pool can get crowded in summer. You can rent lockers, towels and even swimsuits.

The Drive ›› From Radium Hot Springs, it's a lovely 52-mile (83km) drive on Hwy 93 through the park to Ochre Ponds & Paint Pots.

TOP TIP: ROAD CONDITIONS

Weather is very changeable in the mountains. Be sure to carry chains outside of the summer months of June, July and August. Check www.drivebc.ca in BC for current road conditions; in Alberta check www.511.alberta.ca or dial 511.

❷ Ochre Ponds & Paint Pots

As the road delves down into the woods along Hwy 93, a signpost leads to a short, flat interpretive trail. Follow this to the intriguing red-and-orange Ochre Ponds. Drawing Kootenay indigenous groups for centuries – and later European settlers – this iron-rich earth was

LINK YOUR TRIP

2 Around the Kootenays

Continue the adventure through scenic towns by alpine meadows. This epic loop begins in Golden.

3 Icefields Parkway

Join the route in Lake Louise for glacial lakes, untamed forest and world-class wildlife spotting.

collected, mixed with oil and turned into paint. Further along the trail are three stunning crystal-blue springs that are known as the Paint Pots.

The Drive ›› Continue north along Hwy 93 for 1.9 miles (3km) to the next stop.

❸ Marble Canyon

This jaw-dropping stop is not for the faint-of-heart. An easy 15-minute trail zigzags over Tokumm Creek, giving phenomenal views deeper and deeper into Marble Canyon below. The limestone and dolomite walls have been carved away by the awesome power of the creek, resulting in plunging falls and bizarrely shaped cliff faces. The trail can be slippery. Take sturdy shoes and your camera.

The Drive ›› Continue north along Hwy 93 and across the provincial border into Alberta to the junction with Hwy 1 (Castle Junction). Head west.

❹ Banff National Park (p90)

More of a drive than a stop, the stretch of Hwy 1 running from Castle Junction to Lake Louise is one of the most scenic routes through Banff National Park. The highway runs through the Bow Valley, following the weaving Bow River and the route of the Canadian Pacific Railway. The craggy peaks of the giant Sawback and Massive mountain ranges sweep up on either side of the road. The resulting perspective is much wider than on smaller roads with big open vistas.

There are several viewpoint pull-offs where gob-smacked drivers can stop to absorb their surroundings. Watch for the unmissable **Castle Mountain** looming in its crimson glory to the northwest. The Panorama Ridge then rises in the south, after which the enormous **Mt Temple** comes into view, towering at 11,620ft. Stop at the **Mt Temple Viewpoint** for a good gander.

The Drive »» The turnoff for Lake Louise Village is 14.9 miles (24km) from Castle Junction.

- - - - - - - - - - - - - - - - - -

⑤ Lake Louise (p100)

With stunning emerald-green water and tall, snowy peaks that hoist hefty Victoria Glacier up for all to see, Lake Louise has captured the imaginations of mountaineers, artists and visitors for over a century. You – and the enormous numbers of other visitors – will notice the lake's color appears slightly different from each viewpoint.

Follow the **Lakeshore Trail**, a 2.4-mile (4km) round trip, or head up the gorgeous (though somewhat more difficult) route to **Lake Agnes** and its sun-dappled teahouse, perched 4.4 miles (7km) from Lake Louise's shore. For a more relaxed experience, rent a canoe from **Lake Louise Boathouse** (☎403-522-3511; www. fairmont.com/lake-louise/ promotions/canoeing; canoe rental per 30min/1hr $115/125; ☺8am-8:30pm Jun-Sep, weather permitting) and paddle yourself through the icy waters.

Drive back downhill and cross over Hwy 1 to reach the **Lake Louise Gondola** (☎403-522-3555; www.lakelouisegondola.com; 1 Whitehorn Rd; adult/child $38/17; ☺9am-4pm mid-

May–mid-Jun, 8am-5:30pm mid-Jun–Jul, to 6pm Aug, to 5pm Sep–mid-Oct; 👣), which lands you at a lofty 6850ft for a view of the lake and the surrounding glaciers and peaks. En route you'll sail over wildflowers and possibly even a grizzly bear. At the top is the **Wildlife Interpretation Centre**, which hosts regular theater presentations and guided walks.

The Drive »» From Lake Louise Dr, head south along Moraine Lake Rd for 8.7 miles (14km).

- - - - - - - - - - - - - - - - - -

⑥ Moraine Lake

You'll be dazzled by the scenery before you even reach Moraine Lake, set in the Valley of the Ten Peaks. En route, the narrow, winding road gives off fabulous views of the imposing **Wenkchemna Peaks**. Look familiar? For years this scene was carried on the back of the Canadian $20 bill. In 1894, explorer Samuel Allen named the peaks with numbers from one to 10 in the Stoney Indian Language (*wenkchemna* means 'ten'); all but two of the mountains have since been renamed. You'll quickly notice the **Tower of Babel**, ascending solidly toward the heavens at the northeastern edge of the range.

Many people prefer the more rugged and remote setting of Moraine Lake to Lake Louise. The turquoise waters are

DSZC/GETTY IMAGES ©

surprisingly clear for a glacial reservoir. Take a look at the surrounding mountains through telescopes secured to the southern shore (free!) or hire a boat and paddle to the middle for a 360-degree view. There are also some great day hikes from here and, to rest your weary legs, a cafe, dining room and lodge. The road to Moraine Lake and its facilities are open from June to early October.

The Drive »» Return to Hwy 1 and continue west, across the provincial border and into Yoho National Park.

Banff National Park Views of Castle Mountain

❼ Spiral Tunnels

Upon completion of the railway in 1885, trains struggled up the challenging **Kicking Horse Pass**, which you'll cross soon after the Alberta–British Columbia provincial border. This is the steepest railway pass in North America, and wrecks and runaways were common. In 1909 the **Spiral Tunnels** were carved into Mt Cathedral and Mt Ogden and are still in use today. If you time it right, you can see a train exiting from the top of the tunnel while its final cars are still entering at the bottom. Watch from the main viewing area on the north side of the highway.

The Drive ›› Continue west on Hwy 1 and then turn north onto Yoho Valley Rd (open late June to October). This road climbs a number of tight switchbacks.

❽ Takakkaw Falls

Named 'magnificent' in Cree, Takakkaw Falls is one of the highest waterfalls in Canada (804ft). An impressive torrent of water travels from the Daly Glacier, plunges over the edge of the rock face into a small pool and jets out into a tumbling cloud of mist.

En route to the falls you'll pass a second **Spiral Lookout** and the **Meeting of the Rivers**, where the clear Kicking Horse runs into the milky-colored Yoho.

The Drive ›› Return to Hwy 1 and continue west to Field.

❾ Field (p68)

In the midst of Yoho National Park, on the southern side of the Kicking Horse River, lies the quaint village of Field. This historic but unfussy town nestles below a towering mountainscape. While Field may be short on sights, it's a beautiful place to wander around.

DETOUR: BURGESS SHALE WORLD HERITAGE SITE

Start: ⑨ Field

In 1909, Burgess Shale was unearthed on Mt Field. The fossil beds are home to perfectly preserved fossils of marine creatures, dated at least 500 million years old and recognized as some of the earliest forms of life. The area is now a World Heritage site and accessible only by guided hikes, led by naturalists from the **Yoho Shale Geoscience Foundation** (📞800-343-3006; www.burgess-shale.bc.ca; 201 Kicking Horse Ave; tours adult/child from $94.50/65; 🕘9am-4pm Tue-Sat mid-Jun–mid-Sep). Reservations are essential, as is stamina: it's a 12-mile (19.3km) round trip, ascending 2500ft.

Field is also the place to come if you want to organize an activity in the park – from dog-sledding in winter to canoeing and white-water rafting in summer.

The Drive » Continue west on Hwy 1 and take the first right. Continue north for 6.2 miles (10km).

- - - - - - - - - - - - - - - - - -

⑩ Emerald Lake

Gorgeously green Emerald Lake gains its color from light reflecting off fine glacial rock particles that are deposited into the lake by grinding glaciers. It's a highlight of the park, so the lake attracts visitors year-round, either to simply admire its serenity or to fish, skate, hike or horseback ride. In summer, the water warms up just enough to have a very quick dip.

En route to the lake watch for the impressive **natural bridge** stretching across the Kicking Horse River.

The Drive » Return to Hwy 1 and continue to Golden, 33.5 miles (54km) from the turnoff.

- - - - - - - - - - - - - - - - - -

⑪ Golden (p65)

With six national parks in its backyard, little Golden is a popular base. It's also the center for white-water rafting trips on the turbulent Kicking Horse River. Powerful grade III and IV rapids and breathtaking scenery along the sheer walls of Kicking Horse Valley make this rafting experience one of North America's best. Full-day trips on the river are about $159; half-day trips $99. Operators include **Alpine Rafting** (📞250-344-6521; www.alpinerafting.com; 1509 Lafontaine Rd; raft trips from $89; 🕘Jun-Sep; 👪).

More than 60% of the 120 ski runs at **Kicking Horse Mountain Resort** (📞250-439-5425; www.kickinghorseresort.com; Kicking Horse Trail; 1-day lift ticket adult/child winter $94/38, summer $42/21) are rated advanced or expert. It's 8.7 miles (14km) from Golden on Kicking Horse Trail.

The **Northern Lights Wolf Centre** (📞250-344-6798; www.northernlights wildlife.com; 1745 Short Rd; adult/child $12/6; 🕘9am-7pm Jul & Aug, 10am-6pm May, Jun & Sep, noon-5pm Oct-Apr; 🅿) is a refuge for this misunderstood animal, which is being hunted to extinction. Meet a resident wolf or two and learn about their routines and survival.

Takakkaw Falls

Around the Kootenays

With multiple mountain ranges, pockets of mining history and relaxed small towns with idiosyncratic art scenes, BC's Kootenay region is the quiet, unpublicized alternative to the Rocky Mountain national parks.

TRIP HIGHLIGHTS

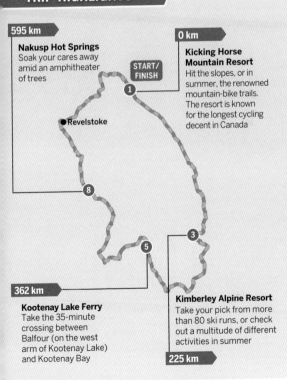

595 km

Nakusp Hot Springs
Soak your cares away amid an amphitheater of trees

● Revelstoke

0 km

Kicking Horse Mountain Resort
Hit the slopes, or in summer, the renowned mountain-bike trails. The resort is known for the longest cycling decent in Canada

START/ FINISH

362 km

Kootenay Lake Ferry
Take the 35-minute crossing between Balfour (on the west arm of Kootenay Lake) and Kootenay Bay

Kimberley Alpine Resort
Take your pick from more than 80 ski runs, or check out a multitude of different activities in summer

225 km

5–6 DAYS
870KM/543 MILES

GREAT FOR...

BEST TIME TO GO
June to September when roads and trails are snow-free and accessible

ESSENTIAL PHOTO
Summit of Mt Revelstoke. ☑**BEST FOR OUTDOORS**
Biking, hiking, and – best of all – whitewater rafting

2 Around the Kootenays

The commanding ranges of the Monashee, Selkirk and Purcell Mountains striate the Kootenays, with the Arrow and Kootenay Lakes adding texture in the middle. This drive allows you to admire their placid alpine meadows and rugged sawtooth ridges while popping into appealing towns such as Revelstoke, Golden, Nelson and Radium Hot Springs in between. Herein lie plenty of launchpads for year-round outdoor adventures.

TRIP HIGHLIGHT

1 Golden (p65)

Golden sits at the confluence of two rivers, three mountain ranges and five national parks – all of them less than 90 minutes drive away.

The town is the center for white-water rafting trips on the turbulent and chilly Kicking Horse River. Along with the powerful grade III and IV rapids, the rugged scenery that guards the sheer walls of the Kicking Horse Val-

ley makes this rafting experience one of North America's best.

Indelibly linked to Golden is the **Kicking Horse Mountain Resort** (📞250-439-5425; www.kickinghorseresort.com; Kicking Horse Trail; 1-day lift ticket adult/child winter $94/38, summer $42/21) 6km to the west – a ski resort that opened in 2000 and is known for its abundance of expert runs. In the summer, the resort and its gondola are handed over to mountain bikers and, more recently, climbers keen to tackle the via ferrata routes.

The Drive » Head south on Hwy 95 through the Columbia River Wetlands, a hugely important ecological area that's home to 260 species of bird and numerous animals, including grizzly bears. In just over an hour, you will arrive in Radium Hot Springs.

---

② Radium Hot Springs (p70)

Lying just outside the southwest corner of Kootenay National Park, Radium Hot Springs is a major gateway to the entire Rocky Mountains national park area.

The town itself isn't much more than a gas and coffee pit-stop. The main attraction is the namesake hot springs, 3km north of town at the jaws of Kootenay National Park (you can hike in via the Sinclair Canyon). One of three hot springs in the Rockies region, Radium is the only one that is odorless. Keeping its water between 37°C and 40°C, the facility is more public baths than fancy spa, although the exposed rock and overhanging trees make for a nice setting.

The Drive » Heading south, Hwy 93/95 follows the wide Columbia River valley between the Purcell and Rocky Mountains. It's not especially interesting, unless you're into the area's industry (ski resort construction), agriculture (golf courses) or wild game (condo buyers). South of Skookumchuck on Hwy 93/95, the road forks. Go right on Hwy 95A and within 30-minutes you'll be in Kimberley.

TRIP HIGHLIGHT

③ Kimberley (p72)

Welcome to Kimberley, a town famous for its erstwhile lead mine, contemporary alpine skiing resort and Canada's largest cuckoo clock.

For well over half a century, Kimberley was home to the world's largest lead-zinc mine, the Sullivan mine, which was finally decommissioned in 2001. Since 2015, the local economy has switched track somewhat and now hosts Canada's largest solar farm.

In the 1970s, Kimberley experimented with a Bavarian theme in the hope of attracting more tourists. Remnants of the Teutonic makeover remain. The central pedestrian zone is named the Platzl and you can still bag plenty of tasty schnitzel and sausages in its restaurants, but these days the town is better known for the **Kimberley Alpine Resort** (📞250-427-4881; www.skikimberley.com; 301 N Star Blvd; 1-day lift pass adult/child $75/30) with 700 hectares of skiable terrain.

For a historical detour, take a 15km ride on **Kimberley's Underground Mining Railway** (📞250-427-7365; www.kimberleysundergroundminingrailway.ca; Gerry Sorensen Way; adult/child $25/10; ⏱tours 11am, 1pm & 3pm May-Sep, trains to resort 10am Sat & Sun),

LINK YOUR TRIP

1 Circling the Rockies

At Radium Hot Springs, divert east onto Hwy 93 which will take you into Kootenay National Park.

3 Icefields Parkway

From Golden, head 84km east to Lake Louise, which marks the beginning of an extraordinary road trip.

where a tiny train putters through the steep-walled Mark Creek Valley toward some sweeping mountain vistas.

The Drive » It's a short 30-minute drive southeast out of Kimberley on Hwy 95A to Cranbrook where you'll merge with Hwy 95 just east of the town.

④ Cranbrook (p72)

The region's main commercial center with a population of just under 20,000, Cranbrook is a modest crossroads. Hwy 3/95 bisects the town, which is a charmless array of strip malls.

The main reason for stopping here is to visit the multifarious **Cranbrook History Centre** (✆250-489-3918; www.

cranbrookhistorycentre.com; 57 Van Horne St S, Hwy 3/95; adult/child $5/3; ⏱10am-5pm Tue-Sun). Dedicated primarily (though not exclusively) to train and rail travel, the center displays some fine examples of classic Canadian trains, including the luxurious 1929 edition of the Trans-Canada Limited, a legendary train that ran from Montréal to Vancouver. Also on-site is a fabulous model railway, the town museum (with plenty of First Nations and pre-human artifacts), and the elegant Alexandra Hall, part of a grand railway hotel that once stood in Winnipeg but was reconstructed in Cranbrook in 2004.

DETOUR: FORT STEELE HERITAGE TOWN

Start ④ Cranbrook

Fort Steele is an erstwhile gold rush town that fell into decline in the early 1900s when it was bypassed by the railway, which went to Cranbrook instead. In the early 1960s, local authorities elected to save the place from total oblivion by turning it into a **heritage site** (✆250-426-7342; www.fortsteele.ca; 9851 Hwy 93/95; adult/youth $18/12 summer; ⏱10am-5pm mid-Jun–Aug, shorter hours winter) of pioneering mining culture. Buildings were subsequently rescued or completely rebuilt in vintage 19th century style to lure in tourists. The site today consists of old shops, stores and a blacksmith, plus opportunities to partake in gold-panning, go on train rides or see a performance in a working theater.

In summer there are all manner of activities and re-creations, which taper off to nothing in winter, although the site stays open.

The Drive » Take Hwy 3 (Crowsnest Hwy) out of Cranbrook. The road is shared with Hwy 95 as far as Yahk, beyond which you pass through the Purcell Mountains to Creston. North of Creston, turn onto Hwy 3A and track alongside the east shore of Kootenay Lake. This leg takes around 2½ hours.

- - - - - - - - - - - - - - - - - -

TRIP HIGHLIGHT

⑤ Kootenay Lake

Lodged in the middle of Kootenays between the Selkirk and Purcell Mountains, Kootenay Lake is one of the largest bodies of freshwater in BC. It's crossed by a year-round toll-free **ferry** (p76) that runs between the two small communities of Kootenay Bay on the east bank, and Balfour on the west. The ferry's a worthwhile side trip if traveling between Creston and Nelson for its long lake vistas of blue mountains rising sharply from the water. Ferries run every 50 minutes throughout the day and the crossing takes 35 minutes. On busy summer weekends, you may have to wait in a long line for a sailing or two before you get passage.

The Drive » From where the ferry disembarks in Balfour on the western shore of Kootenay Lake, take Hwy 3A along the north shore of the West Arm for 32km before crossing the bridge into the town of Nelson.

Radium Hot Springs Bathers enjoy the natural hot pool

6 Nelson (p73)

Nelson is a great reason to visit the Kootenays and should feature on any itinerary in the region. Tidy brick buildings climb the side of a hill overlooking the west arm of deep-blue Kootenay Lake, and the waterfront is lined with parks and beaches. The thriving cafe, culture and nightlife scene is a bonus. But what really propels Nelson is its personality: a mix of hippies, creative types and rugged individualists (many locals will tell you it's the coolest small town in BC). You can find all these along Baker St, the pedestrian-friendly main drag.

Founded as a mining town in the late 1800s, Nelson embarked on a decades-long heritage-preservation project in 1977. Almost a third of Nelson's historic buildings have been restored to their original architectural splendor. Lead yourself on the visitor center's *Heritage Walking Tour*, which gives details on more than 30 buildings and offers a good lesson in Victorian architecture.

The town is also an excellent base for hiking, skiing, kayaking the nearby lakes, and mountain-biking. Free-riding pedal-heads have plenty of favorite spots in British Columbia and the Rockies, but many particularly enjoy Nelson's unique juxtaposition of top-notch single-track and cool bikey ambience. The surrounding area is striped with great trails, from the epic downhill of **Mountain Station** to the winding **Svoboda Road Trails** in West Arm Provincial Park.

The Drive » Heading north from Nelson to Revelstoke, Hwy 6 threads west for 16km before turning north at South Slocan. The road eventually runs alongside pretty Slocan Lake for about 30km before reaching New Denver, 97km from Nelson.

- - - - - - - - - - - - - - - -

7 New Denver (p77)

With only around 500 residents, New Denver is an historic little gem that slumbers away peacefully right on the clear waters of **Slocan Lake**. Chapters in its not-so-sleepy history have included silver mining and a stint as a WWII Japanese internment camp. Details of the former can be found at the **Silvery Slocan Museum** (p77), located in an 1897 Bank of Montreal building.

The Drive » It is a relatively straightforward 46km drive from New Denver to Nakusp on Hwy 6 via Summit Lake Provincial Park. Look out for mountain goats on the rocky outcrops.

- - - - - - - - - - - - - - - -

TRIP HIGHLIGHT

8 Nakusp (p77)

Situated right on Upper Arrow Lake, Nakusp was forever changed by BC's orgy of dam building in the 1950s and 1960s. The water level here was raised and the town was relocated to its current spot, which is why it has a 1960s-era look. It has some attractive cafes and a tiny museum. If

you missed Radium Hot Springs or just can't get enough of the Rocky Mountains' thermal pleasures, divert to **Nakusp Hot Springs** (☎250-265-4528; www.nakusphotsprings.com; 8500 Hot Springs Rd; adult/child $10.50/9.50; ☺9:30am-9:30pm), 12km northeast of town to soak away your cares amid an amphitheater of trees.

The Drive » Head north on Hwy 23 along the east shore of Arrow Lake for 48km. You'll need to cross this lake, too, on a ferry between Galena and Shelter Bay. Hwy 23 continues on the west shore and will take you all the way to Revelstoke, 52km north of Shelter Bay.

- - - - - - - - - - - - - - - -

9 Revelstoke (p62)

Gateway to serious mountains, Revelstoke doesn't need to blow its own trumpet – the ceaseless procession of freight trains through the town center makes more than enough noise. Built as an important point on the Canadian Pacific transcontinental railroad that first linked Eastern and Western Canada, Revelstoke echoes not just with whistles but with history. If you haven't yet been satiated with Canadian railway memorabilia, you can sample a bit more at

the **Revelstoke Railway Museum** (p63).

Revelstoke's compact center is lined with heritage buildings, yet it's more than a museum piece. This place is mainly about the adjacent wilderness and its boundless opportunities for hiking, kayaking and, most of all, skiing. North America's first ski jump was built here in 1915. One year before, Mt Revelstoke became Canada's seventh national park. From the 2223m summit of Mt Revelstoke, the views of the mountains and the Columbia River valley are excellent. To ascend, take the 26km Meadows in the Sky Parkway, 1.6km east of Revelstoke off the Trans-Canada Hwy. Open after the thaw, from mid-May to mid-October, this paved road winds through lush cedar forests and alpine meadows and ends at Balsam Lake, within 2km of the peak. From here, walk to the top or take the free shuttle.

The Drive » Keep your eyes on the road or, better yet, let someone else drive as you traverse the Trans-Canada Hwy (Hwy 1) for 148km between Revelstoke and Golden. Stunning mountain peaks follow one after another as you go.

Icefields Parkway

3

Winding through the wilds of Banff and Jasper National Parks for 230km, the Icefields Parkway offers mesmerizing front-row perspectives on some of North America's most spectacular scenery and wildlife.

TRIP HIGHLIGHTS

202 km

Athabasca Falls
Watch the Athabasca River thunder into its time-sculpted gorge

FINISH
Jasper

9

130 km

Columbia Icefield Discovery Centre
Come face to face with the mighty Athabasca Glacier

7

46 km

Peyto Lake
Glimmering glacial water of an incomparable blue-green hue

Saskatchewan River Crossing

3
2

39 km

Bow Lake
Pristine mountain lake backed by Crowfoot Glacier

Lake Louise
START

2 DAYS
230KM/143 MILES

GREAT FOR

BEST TIME TO GO
June through September for best weather and road conditions

ESSENTIAL PHOTO
The glacial blue-green surface of Peyto Lake

BEST FOR OUTDOORS
Walking on the ice at Athabasca Glacier

3 Icefields Parkway

No North American road trip compares to the Icefields Parkway. Smack along the Continental Divide, this 230km odyssey leads you through one of the least developed stretches of Canada's magnificent Rocky Mountain wilderness. Along the way you'll pass jewel-hued glacial lakes, roaring waterfalls, unbroken virgin forest and a relentless succession of shapely mountain crags, culminating in the awe-inspiring Columbia Icefield. At every turn, spontaneous wildlife sightings are a real possibility.

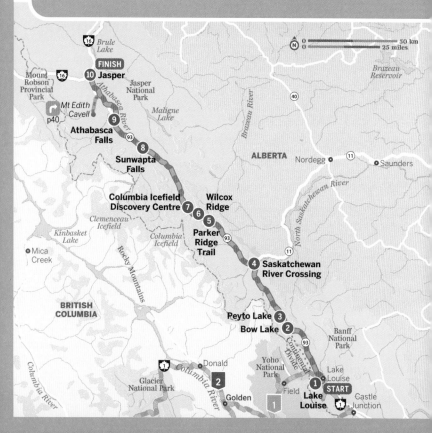

❶ Lake Louise (p100)

Considered by many the crown jewel of Banff National Park, Lake Louise is nearly impossible to describe without resorting to shameless clichés. This serene, implausibly turquoise lake spreads out elegantly below a stately amphitheater of finely sculpted mountains, with Victoria Glacier gleaming high above it all on the opposite shore.

You could easily spend an entire morning gazing at the lake, but anyone with a penchant for hiking should head off to explore the surrounding trails. The most famous leads 4km uphill to the historic **Lake Agnes teahouse** (www.lakeagnes teahouse.com; lunch $7.50-15; ⏱8am-5pm early Jun–early Oct), where you can rejuvenate with scones and hot tea before continuing up to the top of the Big Beehive for spellbinding views back down over blue-green Lake Louise.

The Drive ⟫ Lake Louise sits a stone's throw from the southern entrance to the Icefields Pkwy. Follow the Trans-Canada Hwy a mere 2km west, then take the first exit, purchase (or display) your park entrance pass at the Icefields Pkwy entrance booth, and begin your northward journey into the majestic Rockies, turning left after 37km at the parking lot for Num-Ti-Jah Lodge.

❷ Bow Lake

Ringed by massive peaks and tucked beneath the imposing **Crowfoot Glacier**, Bow Lake is one of the prettiest sights in the Canadian Rockies. Early Banff entrepreneur and wilderness outfitter Jimmy Simpson built his pioneering Num-Ti-Jah Lodge here in 1923 – 12 years before the Icefields Pkwy itself – and it still stands today, its carved-wood interior full to the brim with backcountry nostalgia, animal heads and photos from the golden age.

The hotel changed management and closed its doors in 2021 but could reopen at any time. Check online for updates, if only for its rustic yet elegant **Elkhorn Dining Room** – a top restaurant that let you step back in time to Simpson's world, complete with stone fireplace and majestic views.

The Drive ⟫ Your next stop is just a short 7km up the hill. Get back on the Icefields Pkwy and climb north to Bow Summit. Here, follow the signs on the left for Peyto Lake and park in the first (lower) parking lot.

❸ Peyto Lake

You'll have already seen the indescribably vibrant blue color of Peyto Lake in a thousand publicity shots, but there's nothing like gazing at the real thing – especially since the viewing point for this lake is from a lofty vantage point several hundred feet above the water. The lake gets its extraordinary color from sunlight hitting fine particles of glacial sediment suspended in the water. The lake is best visited in the early morning, between the time the sun first illuminates the water and the first tour bus arrives.

From the bottom of the lake parking lot, follow a paved trail for 15 minutes up a steady gradual incline to the wooden platform overlooking the lake. From here you can return to the parking lot or continue uphill for more fine views from the Bow Summit Lookout trail.

LINK YOUR TRIP

1 Circling the Rockies

Continue exploring Canada's national parks on this scenic ramble through Banff, Kootenay and Yoho. Join the route in Lake Louise.

2 Around the Kootenays

Get off-the-beaten-track amid the small towns and lakes of British Columbia's Monashee, Selkirk and Purcell Mountains. Start in Golden, 84km west of Lake Louise.

The Drive ›› Head north on the Icefields Pkwy and enter the Mistaya Valley watershed. After 16km, pass Waterfowl Lakes on your left, a good place to stretch your legs and soak up more views. Another 19km north, just before Saskatchewan River Crossing, pause on the bridge over the North Saskatchewan River for dramatic views of the river meandering out towards the prairies.

④ Saskatchewan River Crossing

This junction of Hwy 93 (the Icefields Pkwy) and Hwy 11 (the David Thompson Hwy) marks the site where 19th-century fur trappers crossed the North Saskatchewan River on their way through the Rockies to British Columbia. Today, just west of the junction you'll find interpretive historical displays, along with a **motel** (☎403-761-7000; www. thecrossingresort.com; cnr Hwy 11 & Icefields Pkwy; d $229-299; ☺mid-Apr–mid-Oct; P 🛜), restaurant and gas station – the only facilities between Lake Louise and the Columbia Icefield.

The Drive ›› Follow the parkway north along the North Saskatchewan River valley towards an imposing mountain wall. Near the 30km mark, a huge hairpin bend signals the beginning of the ascent to Sunwapta Pass. Stop at the Bridal Veil Falls parking area for fine views back down the valley you're leaving behind. After 38km you'll reach Parker Ridge parking area.

⑤ Parker Ridge Trail

If you only do one hike along the Icefields Pkwy, make it Parker Ridge Trail. It's short enough to crack in an afternoon, but leads to one of the most impressive lookouts of any of Banff's day hikes, with a grandstand view of Mt Saskatchewan, Mt Athabasca and the gargantuan Saskatchewan Glacier. From the parking lot the trail runs through a narrow wood before emerging on the hillside and entering a long series of switchbacks. Crest the ridge at the 2km (1.2-mile) mark, to be greeted by a blast of arctic wind and an explosive panorama of peaks and glaciers.

To the west loom Mts Athabasca and Andromeda, and just to their south is the gleaming bulk of the Saskatchewan Glacier, which lurks at the end of a deep valley. At almost 13km (8 miles) long, the glacier is one of the longest in the Rockies, but it's actually just a spur from the massive 230-sq-km (88-sq-mile) Columbia Icefield that lies to the north. For the best views, follow the trail southeast along the edge of the ridge.

The Drive ›› A short drive northwest on the Icefields Pkwy brings you to your next stop. Shortly after crossing Sunwapta Pass and passing from Banff National Park into Jasper National Park, look for signs for Wilcox Campground on your right and park at the Wilcox Ridge trailhead.

⑥ Wilcox Ridge

One of Jasper's most accessible high country walks is this 9km out-and-back jaunt to Wilcox Ridge. From the trailhead, the path climbs rapidly above the treeline, reaching a pair of red chairs after 30 minutes, where you can sit and enjoy fine Athabasca Glacier views.

If you've had enough climbing, you can simply return from here to the parking lot. Otherwise continue ascending, gazing down over a river canyon on your left as you traverse wide-open

TOP TIP: SPOTTING WILDLIFE

To increase your odds of seeing wildlife, travel the Icefields Pkwy in the early morning or late afternoon. Top areas for wildlife spotting include Tangle Falls (137km north of Lake Louise) and the Goats & Glaciers Viewpoint (195km north of Lake Louise).

meadows to reach Wilcox Pass (2370m) at the 3.2km mark. Here you'll turn left, following the undulating trail another 1.3km to reach the Wilcox Ridge viewpoint. Up top, dramatic, near-aerial views of the Athabasca Glacier unfold across the valley. To return to the parking lot simply retrace your steps downhill.

The Drive » Drive 2.5km west along the Icefields Pkwy to the Columbia Icefield Discovery Centre.

Wilcox Ridge View of the Athabasca Glacier

7 Columbia Icefield Discovery Centre

The massive green-roofed **Columbia Icefield Discovery Centre** (Icefields Pkwy) marks your arrival at the Icefield Pkwy's star attraction, **the Athabasca Glacier**.

The glacier has retreated about 2km since 1844, when it reached the rock moraine on the north side of the road. To reach its toe (bottom edge), walk from the Icefield Centre along the 1.8km Forefield Trail, then join the 1km Toe of the Glacier Trail. You can also park at the start of the latter trail. Visitors are allowed to stand on a small roped section of the ice, should not attempt to cross the warning tape – the glacier is riddled with crevasses.

To walk safely on the Columbia Icefield, you'll need to enlist the help

of **Athabasca Glacier Icewalks** (☎780-852-5595; www.icewalks.com; Icefield Centre; 3hr tour adult/child $110/60, 6hr tour $175/90; ☺late May–Sep), which supplies all the gear you'll need and a guide to show you the ropes. Its basic tour is three hours; there's a six-hour option for those wanting to venture further out onto the glacier.

The other, far easier (and more popular) way to get on the glacier is via the **Columbia Icefield Adventure** (www.banffjasper collection.com/attractions/columbia-icefield; adult/child $114/57; ☺9am-6pm Apr-Oct) tour. A giant all-terrain vehicle known as the Ice Explorer grinds a track onto the ice, where it stops to allow you to go for a 25-minute wander on the glacier. Dress warmly, wear good shoes and bring a water bottle

so you can try some freshly melted glacial water. Tickets can be bought at the Icefield Centre or online; tours depart every 15 to 30 minutes.

Snacks and meals are available at the **Columbia Icefield Discovery Centre dining room** (www. banffjaspercollection.com; Columbia Icefield Discovery Centre; breakfast/lunch buffet $26/33, dinner mains $24-45; ☺ cafeteria 9am-6pm, restaurant 7:30-9:30am, 10:45am-2:45pm & 6-9pm May-Oct), a rather humdrum mall-like affair catering to bus tourists.

The Drive » Begin your long descent down the Athabasca River valley, following the parkway north. Soon after leaving the Columbia Icefield Discovery Centre, watch for Tangle Falls on your right. Bighorn sheep are commonly sighted here. At the 49km mark, follow signs left off the main highway to the Sunwapta Falls parking lot.

WHY THIS IS A CLASSIC TRIP
GREGOR CLARK, WRITER

When I first hitchhiked down the Icefields Parkway on a snowy May morning three days after my 20th birthday, I felt like I had landed on another planet. The endless succession of massive mountains stratified into bands of black rock and white ice filled me with a mixture of awe, joy and terror. Years later, I still react the same way: dwarfed and amazed in the presence of all-powerful, primordial nature.

Above: Parker Ridge Trail
Left: Athabasca Glacier
Right: Sunwapta Falls

AJUMPHOTOGRAPHY/GETTY IMAGES ©

❽ Sunwapta Falls

Meaning 'turbulent water' in the language of the Stoney First Nations, the 18m Sunwapta Falls formed when the glacial meltwaters of the Sunwapta River began falling from a hanging valley into the deeper U-shaped Athabasca Valley. The falls are a magnificent sight as they tumble into a deep narrow gorge; stand on the bridge above for the best views. Afterwards you can stop in for a snack, a meal or an overnight stay at the **Sunwapta Falls Rocky Mountain Lodge** (p92).

The Drive ›› Return to the main highway and drive 24km north. Turn left onto Hwy 93A, following signs for the Athabasca Falls parking area.

❾ Athabasca Falls

Despite being only 23m high, Athabasca Falls is Jasper's most dramatic and voluminous waterfall, a deafening combination of sound, spray and water. The thunderous Athabasca River has cut deeply into the soft limestone rock, carving potholes, canyons and water channels. Interpretive signs explain the basics of the local geology. Visitors crowd the large parking lot and short access trail. It's at its most ferocious during summer.

The Drive ›› You're on the home stretch. A mere 30km jaunt north takes you to Jasper townsite. About 6km before town, you'll cross the Athabasca River and bid farewell to the Icefields Pkwy.

- - - - - - - - - - - - - - - - - -

⑩ Jasper (p104)

With a long and fascinating history that has included fur trappers, explorers, railway workers and some of the Canadian Rockies' earliest tourists, Jasper is the hub town for Jasper National Park. Less than 5000 residents live here year-round, but it feels like a major metropolis after the long journey through the Canadian wilderness. Celebrate with dinner at one of Jasper's diverse selection of eateries: lamb shank or coconut seafood at Raven Bistro, Greek food at **Something Else** (☏780-852-3850; www.somethingelserestaurant.com; 621 Patricia St, Jasper Town;

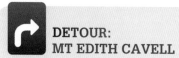

DETOUR:
MT EDITH CAVELL

Start: ⑨ Athabasca Falls

Rising like a snowy sentinel west of the Icefields Pkwy, Mt Edith Cavell (3363m) is one of Jasper National Park's most distinctive and physically arresting peaks. What it lacks in height it makes up for in stark, ethereal beauty. The mountain is famous for its flowery meadows and wing-shaped Angel Glacier.

It was named in honor of a humanitarian British nurse, who was executed by a German firing squad during WWI after helping to smuggle more than 200 wounded Allied soldiers into neutral Holland.

To get here, leave the Icefields Pkwy at the Athabasca Falls turnoff and follow Hwy 93A north 18km, then turn left onto sinuous Edith Cavell Rd, following it until it dead ends at a parking lot. To return to the main route, retrace your steps north on Edith Cavell Rd, then turn left onto Hwy 93A for 5km to its junction with the Icefields Pkwy.

mains $16-40; ⏱11am-11pm), a vegan 'dragon bowl' at **Olive Bistro** (p107), a slow-cooked barbecue at **Maligne Canyon Wilderness Kitchen** (p108) or burgers and microbrews at **Jasper Brewing Co** (p108). Afterwards, settle in for the night at one of the many local cabins or bungalows.

Sunset at Athabasca Falls

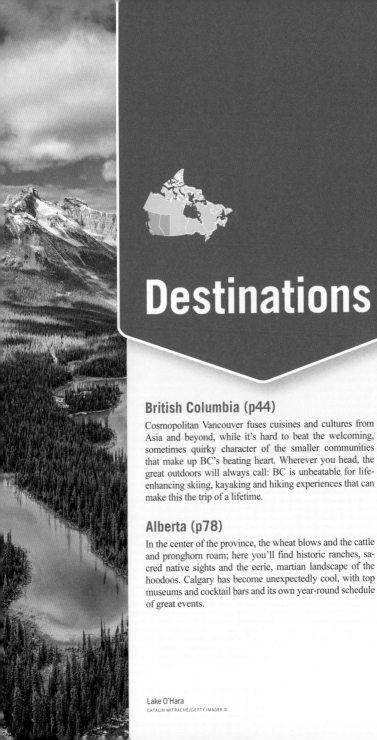

Destinations

British Columbia (p44)

Cosmopolitan Vancouver fuses cuisines and cultures from Asia and beyond, while it's hard to beat the welcoming, sometimes quirky character of the smaller communities that make up BC's beating heart. Wherever you head, the great outdoors will always call: BC is unbeatable for life-enhancing skiing, kayaking and hiking experiences that can make this the trip of a lifetime.

Alberta (p78)

In the center of the province, the wheat blows and the cattle and pronghorn roam; here you'll find historic ranches, sacred native sights and the eerie, martian landscape of the hoodoos. Calgary has become unexpectedly cool, with top museums and cocktail bars and its own year-round schedule of great events.

Lake O'Hara
CATALIN MITRACHE/GETTY IMAGES ©

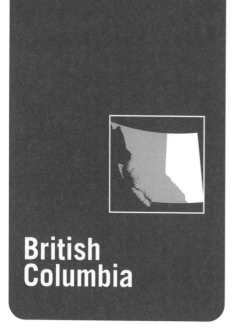

British Columbia

Visitors to Canada's westernmost province should pack a long list of superlatives with them; the words 'wow,' 'amazing' and 'spectacular' will only go so far. Luckily, it's easy to wax lyrical about the mighty mountains, deep forests and dramatic coastlines that instantly lower heart rates to tranquil levels.

ⓘ Getting Around

The sheer size of BC can overwhelm some visitors: it's a scary-sounding 1508km drive from Vancouver to Prince Rupert, for example. While it's tempting to simply stick around Vancouver – the main point of entry for most BC-bound visitors – you won't really have experienced the province unless you head out of town.

Despite the distances, driving remains the most popular method of movement in BC. Plan your routes via the handy DriveBC website (www.drivebc.ca) and check out the dozens of services offered by the extensive BC Ferries (www.bcferries.com) system.

VANCOUVER

♪ 604, 778 / POP 631,500

Explorable neighborhoods, drink-and-dine delights and memorable cultural and outdoor activities framed by striking natural vistas – there's a superfluity of reasons to fall for this ocean-fringed metropolis. But there's much more to Vancouver than downtown.

Walk or hop on public transit and within minutes you'll soon be hanging with the locals in one of the city's diverse and distinctive neighborhoods. Whether discovering the independent boutiques of Main St or the coffee shops of Commercial Dr, the red-brick bars of Gastown or the heritage-house beachfronts of Kitsilano, you'll find this city ideal for easy-access urban exploration. Just be sure to chat to the locals wherever you go: they might seem shy or aloof at first, but Vancouverites love talking up their town and offering their insider tips on stores, bars and restaurants you have to check out.

◉ Sights

Few of Vancouver's main visitor attractions are downtown; the main museums are in Vanier Park and at the University of British Columbia (UBC). Other top sights and landmarks are in Stanley Park or Chinatown, while two major outdoor lures are on the North Shore. Luckily, most are easy to reach by car or transit hop from the city center.

◉ Downtown & West End

★Stanley Park   PARK
(Map p48; www.vancouver.ca/parks; West End; P 🚻; 🚌19) This magnificent 404-hectare park combines excellent attractions with a mystical natural aura. Don't miss a stroll or a cycle (rentals near the W Georgia St entrance) around the 8.8km seawall: a kind of visual spa treatment

fringed by a 150,000-tree temperate rainforest, it'll take you past the park's popular totem poles and along its shimmering oceanfront.

→ Lost Lagoon

This rustic area near Stanley Park's entrance was originally part of Coal Harbour. But after a causeway was built in 1916, the new body of water was renamed, transforming itself into a freshwater lake a few years later. Today it's a **nature sanctuary** – keep your eyes peeled for beady-eyed herons – and its perimeter pathway is a favored stroll for nature-huggers.

→ Stanley Park Seawall

Built between 1917 and 1980, the 8.8km seawall trail is Vancouver's favorite outdoor hangout. Encircling the whole of Stanley Park, it offers spectacular waterfront, mountain-fringed vistas on one side and dense forest canopy on the other. You can walk the whole thing in around hours or rent a bike from the Denman St operators near the entrance to cover the route faster. But what's the rush?

★ Vancouver Art Gallery · · · · · · GALLERY

(Map p48; ☑ 604-662-4700; www.vanartgallery.bc. ca; 750 Hornby St, Downtown; adult/child $24/6.50; ⊙ 10am-5pm Wed-Mon, to 9pm Tue; ⬚5) Combining blockbuster international shows with selections from its striking contemporary collection, the VAG is a magnet for art fans. There are often three or four different exhibitions on its public levels but save time for the top-floor Emily Carr paintings, showcasing swirling nature-themed works from BC's favorite historic artist. Check ahead for FUSE (⊙ 8pm-midnight; $29), a late-opening party with bars and live music. And if you're on a budget, consider the by-donation entry after 5pm on Tuesdays ($10 suggested); expect a queue.

★ Roedde House Museum · · · · · · MUSEUM

(Map p48; ☑ 604-684-7040; www.roeddehouse.org; 1415 Barclay St, West End; $5, Sun $8; ⊙ 1-4pm Tue-Fri & Sun; ⬚5) For a glimpse of what the West End looked like before the apartment blocks, visit this handsome 1893 Queen Anne–style mansion, now a lovingly preserved museum. Designed by infamous architect Francis Rattenbury, the yesteryear, antique-studded rooms have a lived-in feel while its guided tour (included with admission) tells you all about its middle-class Roedde family residents. Look out for the cylinder record player and the taxidermied deer heads that were hunted in Stanley Park in 1906.

Bill Reid Gallery of Northwest Coast Art · · · · · · GALLERY

(Map p48; ☑ 604-682-3455; www.billreidgallery. ca; 639 Hornby St, Downtown; adult/youth/child $13/6/free; ⊙ 10am-5pm May-Sep, 11am-5pm Wed-Sun Oct-Apr; Ⓢ Burrard) Showcasing detailed carvings, paintings, jewelry and more from Canada's most revered Haida artists and others around the region, this open-plan gallery occupies a handsome bi-level hall. Bookended by a totem pole at one end and a ceiling-mounted copper-lined canoe at the other, explore the cabinets of intricate creations and the stories behind them, including some breathtaking gold artifacts. On the mezzanine level, you'll come face-to-face with an 8.5m-long bronze of intertwined magical creatures, complete with impressively long tongues.

Vancouver Aquarium · · · · · · AQUARIUM

(Map p46; ☑ 604-659-3400; www.vanaqua.org; 845 Avison Way, Stanley Park; adult/child $38/21; ⊙ 9:30am-6pm Jul & Aug, 10am-5pm Sep-Jun; ⬚; ⬚19) Stanley Park's biggest draw is home to 9000 critters – including sharks, wolf eels and a somewhat shy octopus. There's also a small, walk-through rainforest area of birds, turtles and a statue-still sloth. The aquarium keeps captive whales and dolphins and organizes animal encounters with these and its other creatures, which may concern some visitors.

Totem poles at Stanley Park

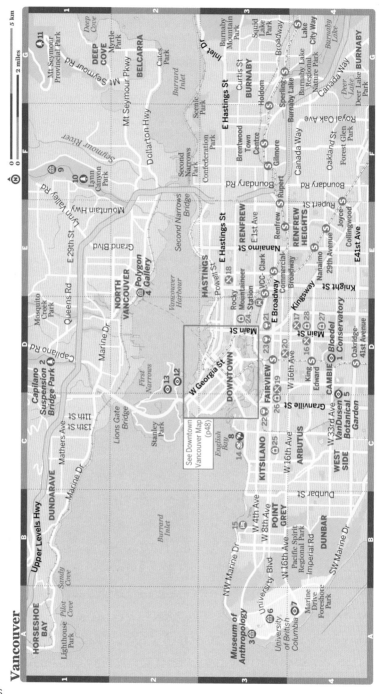

N

0   2 miles
0   5 km

HORSESHOE
BAY

Lighthouse Pilot
Park   Cove

Sandy
Cove

Upper Levels Hwy

DUNDARAVE

Marine Dr

Mathers Ave

Marine Dr

11th St
13th St

Capilano Rd

Capilano
Suspension
Bridge Park 2

Lions Gate
Bridge

Stanley
Park

First
Narrows

English
Bay

Burrard Inlet

Mosquito
Creek
Park

Queens Rd

Marine Dr

NORTH
VANCOUVER

Polygon 4
Gallery

Vancouver
Harbour

W Georgia St

See Downtown
Vancouver Map
(p48)

DOWNTOWN

13

12

Seymour River

E 29th St

Lynn Valley Rd

Mountain Hwy

Grand Blvd

Dollarton Hwy

9

10

Lynn
Canyon
Park

DEEP
COVE

Deep
Cove

Mt Seymour
Provincial Park

11

Mt Seymour Rd

Mt Seymour Pkwy

Myrtle
Park

BELCARRA

Cates
Park

Burrard
Inlet

Second Narrows
Bridge

Second
Narrows
Park

Confederation
Park

Scenic
Park

HASTINGS

Powell St

E Hastings St

18

Rocky
Mountaineer
24 Station

VCC-
Clark

E Hastings St

Curtis St

BURNABY

Holdom

Brentwood
Town
Centre

Gilmore

Sperling

Burnaby Lake

Burnaby
Mountain
Park

Squid
Lake
Park

Broadway

Burnaby Lake
Regional
Nature Park

Deer Lake
Park

BURNABY

City Way

Burnaby
Lake

Deer
Lake

Royal Oak Ave

Canada Way

Boundary Rd

RENFREW

E 1st Ave

Renfrew

Rupert

Rupert St

RENFREW
HEIGHTS

Nanaimo

29th Avenue

Collingwood

E41st Ave

Joyce

Oakland St
Park

Forest Glen
Park

Boundary Rd

Canada Way

Nanaimo St

E Hastings St

KITSILANO

W 4th Ave

25

14

8

W 16th Ave

Dunbar St

POINT
GREY

ARBUTUS

WEST
SIDE

W 33rd Ave

VanDusen
Botanical
Garden

W 16th Ave

W 8th Ave

15

University Blvd

NW Marine Dr

Pacific Spirit
Regional Park

Imperial Rd

SW Marine Dr

DUNBAR

Burrard Inlet

Museum of
Anthropology

6

7

University
of British
Columbia

3

Marine
Drive Foreshore
Park

FAIRVIEW

22

26

19

23

21

17

20

16

28

27

Broadway

E Broadway

Commercial

Main St

Main St

Kingsway

Knight St

Clark

CAMBIE

Bloedel
Conservatory

1

5

Oakridge-
41st Avenue

41st Avenue

King

Edward

Granville St

Cambie

Edmonds

Oakridge

W 16th Ave

Vancouver

Canada Place LANDMARK
(Map p48; ☑ 604-665-9000; www.canadaplace.ca; 999 Canada Place Way, Downtown; 🅿 🚻; Ⓢ Waterfront) FREE Vancouver's version of the Sydney Opera House – judging by the number of postcards it appears on – this iconic landmark is shaped like sails jutting into the sky over the harbor. Both a cruise-ship terminal and a convention center, it's also a stroll-worthy pier, providing photogenic views of the busy floatplane action and looming North Shore mountains. Here for Canada Day on July 1? This is the center of the city's festivities, with displays, live music and fireworks.

◉ Gastown & Chinatown

★**Vancouver Police**
Museum & Archives MUSEUM
(Map p48; ☑ 604-665-3346; www.vancouverpolicemuseum.ca; 240 E Cordova St, Chinatown; adult/child $12/8; ⊙ 9am-5pm Tue-Sat; 🚍 3) Illuminating Vancouver's crime-and-vice-addled history, this quirky museum uncovers the former coroner's courtroom (spot the elaborate cross-hatched ceiling) and sprucing up exhibits including a spine-chilling gallery of real-life cases (weapons included). The star attraction is the old autopsy room, complete with preserved slivers of human tissue; bullet-damaged brain slices are among them. Add a Sins of the City (www.sinsofthecity.ca; adult/student $18/14; ⊙ Apr-Oct; 🚍 14) area walking tour to learn all about Vancouver's salacious olden days; tours include museum entry.

Chinatown Millennium Gate LANDMARK
(Map p48; cnr W Pender & Taylor Sts; Ⓢ Stadium-Chinatown) Inaugurated in 2002, Chinatown's towering entrance is the landmark most visitors look for. Stand well back, since the decoration is mostly on its lofty upper reaches, an elaborately painted section topped with a terra-cotta-tiled roof. The characters inscribed on its eastern front implore you to 'Remember the past and look forward to the future.'

★**Dr Sun Yat-Sen Classical**
Chinese Garden & Park GARDENS
(Map p48; ☑ 604-662-3207; www.vancouverchinesegarden.com; 578 Carrall St, Chinatown; adult/child $14/10; ⊙ 9:30am-7pm mid-Jun–Aug, 10am-6pm Sep & May–mid-Jun, 10am-4:30pm Oct-Apr; Ⓢ Stadium-Chinatown) A tranquil break, this intimate 'garden of ease' reflects Taoist principles of balance and harmony. Entry includes an optional 45-minute guided tour, in which you'll learn about the symbolism behind the placement of the gnarled pine trees, winding covered pathways and ancient limestone formations. Look out for the colorful carp and lazy turtles in the jade-colored water.

Steam Clock LANDMARK
(Map p48; cnr Water & Cambie Sts, Gastown; Ⓢ Waterfront) Halfway along Water St, this oddly popular tourist magnet lures the cameras with its tooting steam whistle. Built in 1977, the clock's mechanism is actually driven by electricity; only the pipes on top are steam fueled (reveal that to the patiently waiting tourists and you might cause a riot). It sounds every 15 minutes, and marks each hour with little whistling symphonies.

Downtown Vancouver

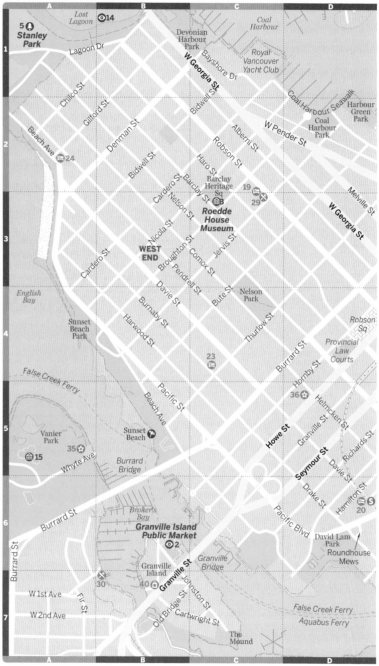

Lost Lagoon

⊙14

5 ⬥ **Stanley Park**

Lagoon Dr

Coal Harbour

Devonian Harbour Park

W Georgia St

Bayshore Dr

Royal Vancouver Yacht Club

Chico St

Gilford St

Bidwell St

Coal Harbour Seawalk

W Pender St

Harbour Green Park

Coal Harbour Park

Beach Ave

⬚24

Denman St

Bidwell St

Alberni St

Robson St

Haro St

Melville St

W Georgia St

Cardero St

Nelson St

Barclay St

Barclay Heritage Sq

19 ⬚

Roedde House Museum

29

Nicola St

WEST END

Broughton St

Jervis St

Comox St

Cardero St

Pendrell St

Davie St

Bute St

Nelson Park

English Bay

Sunset Beach Park

Burnaby St

Harwood St

Thurlow St

Robson Sq

Provincial Law Courts

Burrard St

23
⬚

Hornby St

36 ✪

Helmcken St

Howe St

Granville St

Pacific St

Beach Ave

Vanier Park

35 ✪

⬚15

Whyte Ave

Sunset Beach ⊙

Burrard Bridge

Seymour St

Richards St

Davie St

Drake St

Hamilton St

20 ⑤

False Creek Ferry

Burrard St

Brokers' Bay

Granville Island Public Market

⊙2

Pacific Blvd

David Lam Park

Roundhouse Mews

Burrard St

30

W 1st Ave

Fir St

40 ⬚ **Granville St**

Granville Island

Granville Bridge

Johnston St

Old Bridge St

Cartwright St

False Creek Ferry

Aquabus Ferry

W 2nd Ave

The Mound

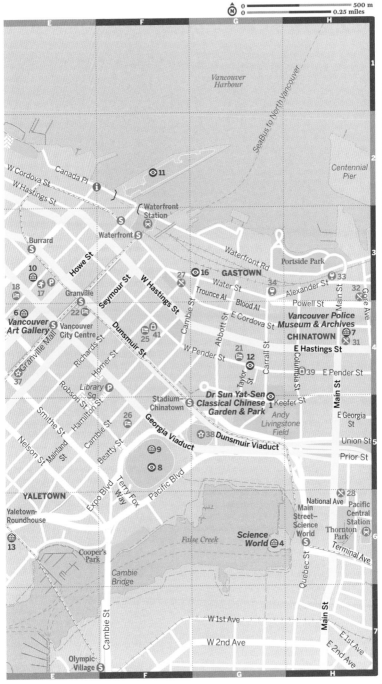

0 500 m
0 0.25 miles

Vancouver
Harbour

SeaBus to North Vancouver

Centennial
Pier

W Cordova St
Canada Pl
W Hastings St

11

Waterfront
Station

Waterfront

Burrard

Howe St

10
18
17

Granville

6 Vancouver
Art Gallery

Granville Mall

22

Vancouver
City Centre

37

Seymour St

W Hastings St

Richards St

Homer St

Robson St

Smithe St

Dunsmuir St

Library
Sq.

Hamilton St

Cambie St

Beatty St

Nelson St

Mainland
St

26

Stadium–
Chinatown

Georgia Viaduct

9

8

YALETOWN

Yaletown-
Roundhouse

13

Expo Blvd

Terry Fox
Way

Cooper's
Park

Cambie
Bridge

Pacific Blvd

Waterfront Rd

Portside Park

27   16   GASTOWN

Water St

Trounce Al

Blood Al

E Cordova St

W Pender St

34

Alexander St

Powell St

33

32

Gore Ave

Vancouver Police
Museum & Archives

CHINATOWN

7

31

E Hastings St

Abbott St

Carrall St

Columbia St

Main St

21
12

Taylor
St

Dr Sun Yat-Sen
Classical Chinese
Garden & Park

Keefer St

Andy
Livingstone
Field

38 Dunsmuir Viaduct

39   E Pender St

Main St

E Georgia
St

Union St

Prior St

False Creek

Science
World   4

National Ave

Main
Street–
Science
World

Thornton
Park

28   Pacific
Central
Station

Quebec St

Terminal Ave

Cambie St

W 1st Ave

W 2nd Ave

Main St

E 1st Ave

E 2nd Ave

Olympic
Village

49

Downtown Vancouver

◉ Yaletown & Granville Island

★**Granville Island Public Market** MARKET
(Map p48; ☑604-666-6655; www.granvilleisland.
com/public-market; Johnston St, Granville Island;
⊙9am-7pm; ☐50, ☑miniferries) The highlight
of Granville Island, this covered market is
a multisensory smorgasbord of fish, cheese,
fruit, teas and bakery treats (near-legendary
Lee's Donuts included). Pick up some fixings
for a picnic at nearby **Vanier Park** or hit the
market's international food court (dine off-
peak and you're more likely to snag a table).
It's not all about food; there are often stands
here hawking all manner of arts and crafts,
from filigree jewelry to knitted baby hats.

Engine 374 Pavilion MUSEUM
(Map p48; www.roundhouse.ca; 181 Roundhouse
Mews, Roundhouse Community Arts & Recreation
Centre, Yaletown; ⊙10am-4pm, reduced hours
off-season; ♿; ⑤Yaletown-Roundhouse) FREE
May 23, 1887, was an auspicious date for Vancouver. That's when Engine 374 pulled the
very first transcontinental passenger train
into the fledgling city, symbolically linking
the country and kick-starting the eventual
metropolis. Retired in 1945, the engine was,
after many years of neglect, restored and
placed in this splendid pavilion. The friendly
volunteers here will show you the best angle
for snapping photos and share a few yesteryear railroading stories at the same time.

BC Sports Hall of Fame & Museum MUSEUM
(Map p48; ☑604-687-5520; www.bcsportshalloffame.
com; 777 Pacific Blvd, Gate A, BC Place Stadium, Yaletown; adult/child $15/12; ⊙10am-5pm; ♿; ⑤Stadium-
Chinatown) Inside **BC Place Stadium** (☑604-
669-2300; www.bcplace.com), this expertly curated attraction showcases top BC athletes, both
amateur and professional, with a fascinating
array of memorabilia. There are medals, tro-
phies and yesteryear sports uniforms on display (judging by the size of their shirts, hockey
players were much smaller in the past), plus
tonnes of hands-on activities to tire the kids
out. Don't miss the **Indigenous Sport Gallery**, covering everything from hockey to la-
crosse to traditional indigenous games.

◉ Main Street

★ Science World
MUSEUM

(Map p48; ☑604-443-7440; www.scienceworld.ca; 1455 Quebec St; adult/child $27.15/18.10; ☺10am-6pm Jul & Aug, reduced hours off-season; Ⓟ♿; ⓢMain St-Science World) Under Vancouver's favorite geodesic dome (OK, it's only one), this ever-popular science showcase has tonnes of hands-on galleries and a cool outdoor park crammed with rugged fun (yes, you *can* lift 2028kg). Inside, there are two floors of brilliant educational play, from plasma balls to whisper dishes. Check out the live critters in the Sara Stern Gallery, the bodily functions exhibits in the BodyWorks area, then fly over a city on the virtual-reality Birdly ride ($8).

◉ Fairview & South Granville

★ VanDusen Botanical Garden
GARDENS

(Map p46; ☑604-257-8335; www.vandusengarden. org; 5251 Oak St; adult/child $11.25/5.50; ☺9am-8pm Jun-Aug, 9am-6pm Apr & Sep, 9am-7pm May, hours reduced Oct-Mar; Ⓟ♿; ◻17) This highly popular green-thumbed oasis is a 22-hectare, 255,000-plant idyll that offers a strollable web of pathways weaving through specialized garden areas: the Rhododendron Walk blazes with color in spring, while the Korean Pavilion is a focal point for a fascinating Asian collection. Save time to get lost in the hedge maze and look out for the herons, owls and turtles that call the park and its ponds home. Informative guided tours are also offered here daily from April to October.

★ Bloedel Conservatory
GARDENS

(Map p46; ☑604-257-8584; www.vandusengarden. org; 4600 Cambie St, Queen Elizabeth Park; adult/child $6.75/3.30; ☺10am-5pm Jan-Mar, Nov & Dec, 10am-6pm Apr, Sep & Oct, 10am-8pm May-Aug; Ⓟ♿; ◻15) Cresting the hill in Queen Elizabeth Park, this domed conservatory is a delightful rainy-day warm-up. At Vancouver's best-value paid attraction, you'll find tropical trees and plants bristling with hundreds of free-flying, bright-plumaged birds. Listen for the noisy resident parrots but also keep your eyes peeled for rainbow-hued Gouldian finches, shimmering African superb starlings and maybe even a dramatic Lady Amherst pheasant, snaking through the undergrowth.

◉ Kitsilano & University of British Columbia

★ Museum of Anthropology
MUSEUM

(MOA; Map p46; ☑604-822-5087; www.moa.ubc. ca; 6393 NW Marine Dr, UBC; adult/child $18/16; ☺10am-5pm Fri-Wed, 10am-9pm Thu, closed Mon Oct-May; Ⓟ; ◻99B-Line, then 68) Vancouver's best museum is studded with spectacular indigenous totem poles and carvings – but it's also teeming with artifacts from cultures around the world, from intricate Swedish lace

DEYMOSHR/SHUTTERSTOCK ©

Granville Island Public Market

to bright Sri Lankan folk masks. Take one of the free daily tours (check ahead for times) for some context, but give yourself at least a couple of hours to explore on your own; it's easy to immerse yourself here. On a budget? Thursday evening entry is $10 (after 5pm).

Kitsilano Beach BEACH

(Map p46; cnr Cornwall Ave & Arbutus St, Kitsilano; 🚌2) Facing English Bay, Kits Beach is one of Vancouver's favorite summertime hangouts. The wide, sandy expanse attracts buff Frisbee tossers, giggling volleyball players and those who just like to preen while catching the rays. The ocean is fine for a dip, though serious swimmers should consider the heated **Kitsilano Pool** (☑604-731-0011; www.vancouverparks.ca; 2305 Cornwall Ave; adult/child $6.10/3.05; ⏰7am-evening mid-Jun–Sep; 🅿; 🚌2), one of the world's largest outdoor saltwater pools.

Museum of Vancouver MUSEUM

(MOV; Map p48; ☑604-736-4431; www.museumofvancouver.ca; 1100 Chestnut St, Kitsilano; adult/child $20.50/9.75; ⏰10am-5pm Sun-Wed, to 8pm Thu, to 9pm Fri & Sat; 🅿👶; 🚌2) The MOV serves up cool temporary exhibitions alongside in-depth permanent galleries of fascinating First Nations artifacts and evocative pioneer-era exhibits. But it really comes to life in its vibrant 1950s pop culture and 1960s hippie counterculture sections, a reminder that Kitsilano was once the grass-smoking center of Vancouver's flower-power movement. Don't miss the shimmering gallery of vintage neon signs collected from around the city; it's a favorite with locals.

Beaty Biodiversity Museum MUSEUM

(Map p46; ☑604-827-4955; www.beatymuseum.ubc.ca; 2212 Main Mall, UBC; adult/child $14/10; ⏰10am-5pm Tue-Sun; 👶; 🚌99B-Line) A family-friendly museum showcasing a two-million-item natural-history collection including birds, fossils and herbarium displays. The highlight is the 25m blue-whale skeleton, artfully displayed in the two-story entranceway. Don't miss the first display case, which is crammed with a beady-eyed menagerie of tooth-and-claw taxidermy. Consider visiting on the third Thursday of the month when entry is by donation after 5pm and the museum stays open until 8:30pm; there's often a special theme or live performance for these monthly Nocturnal events.

UBC Botanical Garden GARDENS

(Map p46; ☑604-822-4208; www.botanicalgarden.ubc.ca; 6804 SW Marine Dr, UBC; adult/child $10/5; ⏰10am-4:30pm; 👶; 🚌99B-Line, then 68) You'll find a huge array of rhododendrons, a fascinating apothecary plot and a winter green space of off-season bloomers in this 28-hectare complex of themed gardens. Among the towering trees, look for northern flicker woodpeckers and chittering little Douglas squirrels. Also save time for the attraction's **Greenheart TreeWalk** (adult/child $23/10; ⏰Apr-Oct), which elevates visitors up to 23m above the forest floor on a 310m guided ecotour. The combined garden and Greenheart ticket costs adult/child $23/10.

HR MacMillan Space Centre MUSEUM

(Map p48; ☑604-738-7827; www.spacecentre.ca; 1100 Chestnut St, Kitsilano; adult/child $19.50/14; ⏰10am-5pm Jul & Aug, reduced hours off-season; 🅿👶; 🚌2) Focusing on the wonderful world of space, admission to this kid-favorite museum includes a gallery of hands-on exhibits (don't miss the Mars section where you can drive across the surface in a simulator) as well as a menu of live science demonstrations in the small theater and a cool 45-minute planetarium show upstairs. Check the daily schedule of shows and presentations online before you arrive. The Saturday-night planetarium performances are popular with locals and typically draw a more adult crowd.

◉ North Shore

⭐**Capilano Suspension Bridge Park** PARK

(Map p46; ☑604-985-7474; www.capbridge.com; 3735 Capilano Rd, North Vancouver; adult/child $47/15; ⏰8am-8pm May-Aug, reduced hours off-season; P 🚻; 🚌236) As you inch gingerly across one of the world's longest (140m) and highest (70m) pedestrian suspension bridges, swaying gently over roiling Capilano Canyon, remember that its thick steel cables are firmly embedded in concrete. That should steady your feet – unless there are teenagers stamping across. Added park attractions include a glass-bottomed cliffside walkway and an elevated canopy trail through the trees.

★ **Polygon Gallery**   GALLERY
(Map p46; 🖉604-986-1351; www.thepolygon.ca; 101 Carrie Cates Ct, North Vancouver; by donation; ⊗10am-5pm Tue-Sun; 🚢Lonsdale Quay SeaBus) This dramatic, sawtooth-roofed waterfront landmark stages multiple exhibitions throughout the year. Photoconceptualism remains a focus but expect thought-provoking contemporary art installations and evocative Aboriginal exhibits as well. There are free 45-minute tours every Saturday at 2pm. The small, yet highly interesting Museum of North Vancouver opened across the street in 2021.

Lynn Canyon Park   PARK
(Map p46; www.lynncanyon.ca; Park Rd, North Vancouver; ⊗10am-5pm Jun-Sep, noon-4pm Oct-May; P 🚻; 🚌228 then 227) FREE Amid a dense bristling of century-old trees, the main lure of this popular park is its Suspension Bridge, a free alternative to Capilano. Not quite as big as its tourist-magnet rival, it nevertheless provokes the same jelly-legged reaction as you sway over the river that tumbles 50m below – and it's always far less crowded. Hiking trails, swimming areas and picnic spots will keep you busy, while there's also a cafe to fuel up.

The park's Ecology Centre (🖉604-990-3755; www.lynncanyonecologycentre.ca; 3663 Park Rd; by donation; ⊗10am-5pm Jun-Sep, 10am-5pm Mon-Fri & noon-4pm Sat & Sun Oct-May; 🚻; 🚌227) 🖉 houses interesting displays, including dioramas on the area's rich biodiversity. There are also some fascinating free history-themed walking tours in the park on Wednesdays and Thursdays in July and August; check www.nvma.ca/programs for details.

Mt Seymour Provincial Park   PARK
(Map p46; www.bcparks.ca; 1700 Mt Seymour Rd, North Vancouver; ⊗dawn-dusk) A popular rustic retreat from the downtown clamor, this huge, tree-lined park is suffused with summertime hiking trails that suit walkers of most abilities (the easiest path is the 2km Goldie Lake Trail). Many trails wind past lakes and centuries-old Douglas firs. This is also one of the city's main winter playgrounds.

🏃 **Activities & Tours**

Vancouver's variety of outdoorsy activities is a huge hook: you can ski in the morning and hit the beach in the afternoon; hike or bike scenic forests; paddleboard along the coastline; or kayak to your heart's content – and it will be content, with grand mountain views as your backdrop. There's also a full menu of spectator sports to catch here.

★ **Grouse Mountain**   SNOW SPORTS
(🖉604-980-9311; www.grousemountain.com; 6400 Nancy Greene Way, North Vancouver; lift ticket adult/child $47/42; ⊗9am-10pm mid-Nov–mid-Apr; 🚻; 🚌236) Vancouver's favorite winter hangout, family-friendly Grouse offers four chairlifts plus 33 ski and snowboard runs (including night runs). Classes and lessons are available for beginners and beyond, and the area's forested snowshoe trails are magical. There are also a couple of dining options if you just want to relax and watch the snow with a hot chocolate in hand.

If you're here in December, this is a great place to soak up some Christmas spirit.

★ **Cycle City Tours**   CYCLING
(Map p48; 🖉604-618-8626; www.cyclevancouver.com; 648 Hornby St, Downtown; tours from $65, bicycle rentals per hour/day $9.50/38; ⊗9am-6pm, reduced hours in winter; 🚇Burrard) Striped with bike lanes, Vancouver is a good city for two-wheeled exploring. But if you're not great at navigating, consider a guided tour with this popular operator. Its Grand Tour ($90) is a great city intro, while the Craft Beer Tour ($90) includes brunch and three breweries. Alternatively, go solo with a rental; there's a bike lane outside the store.

★ **Vancouver Foodie Tours** TOURS
(☎604-295-8844; www.foodietours.ca; tours from $65) A popular culinary-themed city stroll operator running three tasty tours in Vancouver; choose between Best of Downtown, Gastronomic Gastown and Granville Island tours. Friendly red-coated guides lead you on belly-pleasing ventures with plenty to eat and drink; the trick is not to dine before you arrive.

Festivals & Events

Vancouver Craft Beer Week BEER
(www.vancouvercraftbeerweek.com; event tickets from $15; ⊙late May) A showcase for BC's amazing craft-beer scene, with dozens of tasty events around the city.

Vancouver International Jazz Festival MUSIC
(www.coastaljazz.ca; ⊙Jun) City-wide cornucopia of superstar shows and free outdoor events from mid-June.

Pride Week LGBTIQ+
(www.vancouverpride.ca; West End; ⊙Aug) Parties, concerts and fashion shows, as well as the city's biggest annual street parade.

Pacific National Exhibition CULTURAL
(PNE; www.pne.ca; 2901 E Hastings St, Hastings Park; adult/under-13s $18/free; ⊙mid-Aug–Sep; 👪; 🚌14) Family-friendly shows, music concerts and fairground fun (plus lots of calorific things to eat).

Eastside Culture Crawl ART
(www.culturecrawl.ca; ⊙mid-Nov) Vancouver's best visual-arts festival: a four-day gallery and studio open house with hundreds of participants.

URBAN BIRDING

You don't have to go far to spot some beady-eyed locals in this city. Birding has become a popular pastime for many Vancouverites and if you're keen to join in the feather-fancying fun, consider spending an hour or two in Stanley Park (p44), **Vanier Park**, **Pacific Spirit Park** or **Queen Elizabeth Park**. Many city streets are also lined with established trees that are home to a surprisingly diverse array of beaked critters: on our West End exploration, we spotted hummingbirds, barred owls and northern flicker woodpeckers. Heading into adjoining Stanley Park, you might also see wrens, chickadees, downy woodpeckers, bald eagles, coots, ducks, cormorants and herons – which are also famous for nesting in a large and noisy heronry here every spring.

Sleeping

Metro Vancouver is home to more than 23,000 hotel, B&B and hostel rooms, the majority in or around the downtown core. Airbnb also operates here, although a regulatory crackdown has reduced their number in recent years. Book far ahead for summer or you may struggle to find a place to lay your head. Rates peak in July and August, but there are good spring and fall deals here (alongside increased rainy days).

YWCA Hotel HOTEL $
(Map p48; ☎604-895-5830; www.ywcahotel.com; 733 Beatty St, Yaletown; s/d/tr without bath $106/118/173; P⊖❄@📶; SStadium-Chinatown) A good-value, well-located option with nicely maintained (if spartan) rooms of the student-accommodations variety. There's a range of configurations, from singles to five-bed rooms, plus shared, semiprivate or private bathrooms. Each room has a TV and mini-refrigerator and there are TV lounges and communal kitchens too. Rates include access to the YWCA Health & Fitness Centre, a 15-minute walk away.

HI Vancouver Jericho Beach HOSTEL $
(Map p46; ☎604-224-3208; www.hihostels.com; 1515 Discovery St, Kitsilano; dm/d $43/86; ⊙May-Sep; P@📶; 🚌4) One of Canada's largest hostels looks like a Victorian hospital but has a scenic near-the-beach location. Basic rooms make this the least palatial Vancouver HI hostel, but it has a large kitchen, bike rentals and a popular licensed cafe. Dorms are also larger here. Book ahead for the popular budget-hotel-style private rooms (with shared and private bathroom options).

★ **Victorian Hotel** HOTEL $$
(Map p48; ☎604-681-6369; www.victorianhotel.ca; 514 Homer St, Downtown; d incl breakfast from $200; ⊖@📶; SGranville) The high-ceilinged rooms at this well-maintained heritage hotel combine glossy hardwood floors, a sprinkling of antiques, an occasional bay window and plenty of historical charm. The best rooms are in the extension, where raindrop

showers, marble bathroom floors and flat-screen TVs add a slice of luxe. Rates include continental breakfast and rooms are provided with fans in summer.

★ Sunset Inn & Suites
HOTEL **$$**

(Map p48; ☑604-688-2474; www.sunsetinn.com; 1111 Burnaby St, West End; d incl breakfast $225; P❄@🛜; 🚌6) A good-value cut above most of Vancouver's self-catering suite hotels, the popular Sunset Inn offers larger-than-average rooms with kitchens. Each has a balcony, and some – particularly those on south-facing higher floors – have partial views of English Bay. Rates include continental breakfast (with make-your-own waffles) and, rare for Vancouver, free parking. The attentive staff is among the best in the city.

★ Skwachàys Lodge
BOUTIQUE HOTEL **$$**

(Map p48; ☑604-687-3589; www.skwachays.com; 29 W Pender St, Chinatown; d from $300; ❄🛜; Ⓢ Stadium-Chinatown) The 18 small but elegantly designed rooms at this sparkling First Nations art hotel include the captivating Forest Spirits Suite, with floor-to-ceiling birch branches, and the sleek Longhouse Suite, with its illuminated metalwork frieze. Deluxe trappings such as ecofriendly toiletries are standard and there's an on-site gallery for purchasing one-of-a-kind artworks.

Sylvia Hotel
HOTEL **$$**

(Map p48; ☑604-681-9321; www.sylviahotel.com; 1154 Gilford St, West End; d from $199; P@🛜❄; 🚌5) This ivy-covered 1912 charmer enjoys a prime location overlooking English Bay. Generations of guests keep coming back – many requesting the same room every year – for a dollop of old-world ambience, plus a side order of first-name service. The rooms, some with older furnishings, have an array of comfortable configurations; the best are the large suites with kitchens and waterfront views.

St Regis Hotel
BOUTIQUE HOTEL **$$$**

(Map p48; ☑604-681-1135; www.stregishotel.com; 602 Dunsmuir St, Downtown; d incl breakfast from $325; ❄@🛜; Ⓢ Granville) An elegant art-lined boutique sleepover in a 1913 heritage shell. Befitting its age, almost all the rooms seem to be a different size, and they exhibit a loungey élan with deco-esque furniture, earth-toned bedspreads, flat-screen TVs and multimedia hubs. Rates include value-added flourishes such as cooked breakfasts, access to the nearby gym and free long-distance and international phone calls.

VANCOUVER'S BEST BLOGS

Miss 604 (www.miss604.com) Vancouver's leading blogger, covering local events and happenings.

Scout Magazine (www.scoutmagazine. ca) Trendy site profiling the city's food and drinks scene.

Bored in Vancouver (www.boredinvancouver.com) Alternative take on multiple scenes around the city.

Daily Hive Vancouver (www.dailyhive. com/vancouver) City news and lifestyle happenings.

Listel Hotel
BOUTIQUE HOTEL **$$$**

(Map p48; ☑604-684-8461; www.thelistelhotel. com; 1300 Robson St, West End; d from $340; P❄@🛜; 🚌5) ✦ A lounge-cool sleepover with famously friendly front-deskers. Rooms have a relaxed West Coast feel and typically feature striking original artworks. But it's not all about looks; cool features include glass water bottles in the rooms, a daily wine reception (from 5pm) and the free use of loaner e-bikes if you want to explore nearby Stanley Park).

Fairmont Hotel Vancouver
HOTEL **$$$**

(Map p48; ☑604-684-3131; www.fairmont.com/ hotel-vancouver; 900 W Georgia St, Downtown; d from $500; P❄@🛜❄❄; Ⓢ Vancouver City Centre) Opened in 1939 by visiting UK royals, this gargoyle-topped grand dame is a Vancouver historic landmark. Despite its vintage provenance, the hotel carefully balances comfort with elegance; the lobby is bedecked with crystal chandeliers but the rooms have an understated business-hotel feel. If you have the budget, check into the Gold Floor for a raft of pampering extras.

Opus Hotel
BOUTIQUE HOTEL **$$$**

(Map p48; ☑604-642-6787; www.opushotel.com; 322 Davie St, Yaletown; d $500; P❄🛜❄; Ⓢ Yaletown-Roundhouse) The 96-room Opus kick-started Vancouver's boutique-hotel scene and, with regular revamps, it's remained one of the city's top sleepover options. The designer rooms have contemporary-chic interiors with bold colors, mod furnishings and feng-shui bed placements, while many of the luxe bathrooms have clear windows overlooking the streets (visiting exhibitionists take note).

✗ Eating

Vancouver has an eye-popping array of gen-erally good-value dine-out options: authen-tic Asian restaurants, finger-licking brunch spots, fresh-catch seafood joints and a lo-cally sourced farm-to-table scene are all on the menu here. You don't have to be a local to indulge: just follow your taste buds and dinner will become the most talked-about highlight of your Vancouver visit.

★ Ovaltine Cafe   DINER $
(Map p48; ☑ 604-685-7021; www.facebook.com/ ovaltinecafe; 251 E Hastings St, Chinatown; mains $7-10; ☺ 6:30am-3pm Mon-Sat, 6:30am-2pm Sun; ☐ 14) Like being inside Edward Hop-per's *Nighthawks* diner painting, this time-capsule greasy spoon instantly transports you to the 1940s. Snag a booth alongside the hospital-green walls or, better yet, slide onto a tape-repaired spinning stool at the long counter. Truck-stop coffee is de rigueur here, alongside burgers, sandwiches and fried breakfasts that haven't changed in decades (yes, that's liver and onions on the menu).

★ Go Fish   SEAFOOD $
(Map p48; ☑ 604-730-5040; 1505 W 1st Ave; mains $8-14; ☺ 11:30am-6pm Mon-Fri, noon-6pm Sat & Sun; ☐ 50) A short stroll westward along the seawall from the Granville Island entrance, this almost-too-popular seafood stand is one of the city's fave fish-and-chip joints, offering halibut, salmon and cod encased in crispy golden batter. The smashing fish tacos are also recommended, while chang-ing daily specials – brought in by the nearby fishing boats – often include scallop burgers or ahi tuna sandwiches.

★ Caffè La Tanna   ITALIAN $
(Map p46; ☑ 604-428-5462; www.caffelatana. ca; 635 Commercial Dr; mains $12-16; ☺ 8am-6pm; ☐ 20) Like a 1950s neighborhood cafe in Rome, this handsome little hidden gem looks like it's been here for decades. But it's a nice addition to this quiet stretch of the Drive, luring delighted locals with its deli-cate housemade pastries and fresh pastas (watch the mesmerizing pasta production at the counter). Check the daily special and peruse the shelves of Italian groceries, too.

★ Forage   CANADIAN $$
(Map p48; ☑ 604-661-1400; www.foragevancouver. com; 1300 Robson St, West End; mains $16-35; ☺ 6:30-10am & 5-11pm Mon-Fri, 7am-2pm & 5-11pm Sat & Sun; 🔊; ☐ 5) 🍃 A popular farm-to-table

eatery, this sustainability-focused restaurant is the perfect way to sample regional flavors. Brunch has become a firm local favorite (halibut eggs Benny recommended), and for dinner there's everything from bison steaks to slow-cooked salmon. Add a flight of BC craft beers, with top choices from the likes of Four Winds, Strange Fellows and more. Reservations recommended.

★ Campagnolo   ITALIAN $$
(Map p48; ☑ 604-484-6018; www.campagnolores taurant.ca; 1020 Main St, Chinatown; mains $18-25; ☺ 11:30am-2:30pm Mon-Fri, plus 5:30-10pm daily; 🍴; ☐ 3) Eyebrows were raised when this contemporary, rustic-style Italian res-taurant opened in a hitherto sketchy part of town. But Campagnolo has lured locals and inspired a miniwave of other restaurants in the vicinity. Reserve ahead and dive into reinvented comfort dishes such as shrimp gnocchetti and a fennel sausage-topped pizza that may induce you to eat your body weight in thin-crust.

★ Anh & Chi   VIETNAMESE $$
(Map p46; ☑ 604-878-8883; www.anhandchi. com; 3388 Main St; mains $16-25; ☺ 11am-11pm; 🍴; ☐ 3) You'll find warm and solicitous service at this delightful contemporary Vi-etnamese restaurant whose authentic, per-fectly prepared dishes are a must for local foodies. Not sure what to order? Check out the menu's 'bucket list' dishes, including the highly recommended prawn-and-pork-packed crunchy crepe. Reservations are not accepted and waits here can be long; consid-er mid-afternoon weekday dining instead.

★ Acorn   VEGETARIAN $$
(Map p46; ☑ 604-566-9001; www.theacornrestau rant.ca; 3995 Main St; mains $18-22; ☺ 5:30-10pm Mon-Thu, to 11pm Fri, 10am-2:30pm & 5:30-11pm Sat, to midnight Sun; 🍴; ☐ 3) One of Vancou-ver's hottest vegetarian restaurants – hence the sometimes long wait for tables – the Acorn is ideal for those craving something more inventive than mung-bean soup. Con-sider seasonal, artfully presented treats such as beer-battered haloumi or vanilla-al-mond-beet cake and stick around at night: the bar serves until midnight if you need to pull up a stool and set the world to rights.

★ Salmon n' Bannock   NORTHWESTERN US $$
(Map p46; ☑ 604-568-8971; www.facebook.com/ SalmonNBannockBistro; 1128 W Broadway, Fairview; mains $16-32; ☺ 5-10pm Mon-Sat; ☐ 9) Vancou-

ver's only First Nations restaurant is an utterly delightful art-lined little bistro on an unassuming strip of Broadway shops. It's worth the easy bus trip, though, for fresh-made indigenous-influenced dishes made with local ingredients. The juicy salmon 'n' bannock burger has been a staple here for years but more elaborate, feast-like options include game sausages and bison pot roast.

★**St Lawrence Restaurant**　　　FRENCH $$$
(Map p48; ☑604-620-3800; www.stlawrenceres-taurant.com; 269 Powell St, Railtown; mains $34-44; ⊙5:30-10:30pm Tue-Sun; ◻4) Resembling a handsome wood-floored bistro that's been teleported straight from Montréal, this sparkling, country-chic dining room is a Railtown superstar. The Québecois approach carries over onto a small menu of elevated, perfectly prepared old-school mains such as trout in brown-butter sauce and the utterly delicious duck-leg confit with sausage. French-Canadian special-occasion dining at its finest.

★**Vij's**　　　INDIAN $$$
(Map p46; ☑604-736-6664; www.vijs.ca; 3106 Cambie St, Cambie Village; mains $23-36; ⊙5:30-10pm; ☑; ◻15) Spicy aromas scent the air as you enter this warmly intimate dining space for Vancouver's finest Indian cuisine. Exemplary servers happily answer menu questions, while bringing over snacks and chai tea. There's a one-page array of tempting dishes but the trick is to order three or four to share (mains are all available as small plates and orders come with rice and naan).

🍺 Drinking & Nightlife

Vancouverites spend a lot of time drinking. And while BC has a tasty wine sector and is undergoing an artisanal distilling surge, it's the regional craft-beer scene that keeps many quaffers merry. For a night out with locally made libations as your side dish, join savvy city drinkers in the bars of Gastown, Main St and beyond.

★**Alibi Room**　　　PUB
(Map p48; ☑604-623-3383; www.alibi.ca; 157 Alexander St, Gastown; ⊙5-11:30pm Mon-Thu, 5pm-12:30am Fri, 10am-12:30am Sat, 10am-11:30pm Sun; 🛜; ◻4) Vancouver's best craft-beer tavern pours a near-legendary roster of 50-plus drafts, many from celebrated BC breweries including Four Winds, Yellow Dog and Dageraad. Hipsters and veteran-ale fans alike love

the 'frat bat': choose your own four samples or ask to be surprised. Check the board for new guest casks and stick around for a gastropub dinner at one of the long communal tables.

★**Grapes & Soda**　　　WINE BAR
(Map p46; ☑604-336-2456; www.grapesandsoda.ca; 1541 W 6th Ave, South Granville; ⊙5:30-11pm Tue-Sat; ◻10) A warm, small-table hangout that self-identifies as a 'natural wine bar' (there's a well-curated array of options from BC, Europe and beyond). This local favorite also serves excellent cocktails: from the countless bottles behind the small bar, they can seemingly concoct anything your taste buds desire, whether or not it's on the menu. Need help? Slide into a Scotch, ginger and walnut Cortejo.

★**Key Party**　　　BAR
(Map p46; www.keyparty.ca; 2303 Main St; ⊙5pm-1am Mon-Thu, to 2am Fri & Sat, to 1am Sun; ◻3) Walk through the doorway of a fake storefront that looks like an accountancy office and you'll find yourself in a candlelit, boudoir-red speakeasy dominated by a dramatic mural of frolicking women and animals. Arrive early to avoid the queues, then fully explore the entertaining cocktail program (Kir Royale champagne jello shooters included).

★**Brassneck Brewery**　　　MICROBREWERY
(Map p46; ☑604-259-7686; www.brassneck.ca; 2148 Main St; ⊙2-11pm Mon-Fri, noon-11pm Sat & Sun; ◻3) A beloved Vancouver microbrewery with a small, wood-lined tasting room. Peruse the ever-changing chalkboard of intriguing libations with names such as Pinky Promise, Silent Treatment and Faux Naive, or start with a delicious, highly accessible Passive Aggressive dry-hopped pale ale. It's often hard to find a seat here, so consider a weekday afternoon visit for a four-glass $8 tasting flight.

★**Guilt & Co**　　　BAR
(Map p48; www.guiltandcompany.com; 1 Alexander St, Gastown; ⊙7pm-late; ⑤Waterfront) This cavelike subterranean bar, beneath Gastown's brick-cobbled sidewalks, is also a brilliant venue to catch a tasty side dish of live music. Most shows are pay-what-you-can and can range from trumpet jazz to heartfelt singer-songwriters. Drinks-wise, there's a great cocktail list plus a small array of draft beers (and many more in cans and bottles). Avoid weekends when there are often long queues.

☆ Entertainment

★ Commodore Ballroom
LIVE MUSIC

(Map p48; ☎ 604-739-4550; www.commodoreball-room.com; 868 Granville St, Downtown; tickets from $30; 🚇10) Local bands know they've made it when they play Vancouver's best mid-sized venue, a restored art-deco ballroom that still has the city's bounciest dance floor – courtesy of tires placed under its floorboards. If you need a break from moshing, collapse at one of the tables lining the perimeter, catch your breath with a bottled brew and then plunge back in.

★ Arts Club Theatre Company
THEATER

(☎604-687-1644; www.artsclub.com; tickets from $29; ⊙Sep-Jun) Vancouver's largest, most popular and most prolific theater company, the Arts Club stages shows at three venues around the city.

★ Bard on the Beach
PERFORMING ARTS

(Map p48; ☎604-739-0559; www.bardonthebeach.org; 1695 Whyte Ave, Vanier Park, Kitsilano; tickets from $24; ⊙Jun-Sep; ♿; 🚇2) Watching Shakespeare performed while the sun sets over the mountains beyond the tented main stage is a Vancouver summertime highlight. There are usually three Shakespeare plays, plus one Bard-related work (*Rosencrantz and Guildenstern are Dead,* for example), to choose from during the season. Q&A talks are staged after some Tuesday performances; also opera, fireworks and wine-tasting special nights are held throughout the season.

★ Cinematheque
CINEMA

(Map p48; ☎604-688-8202; www.thecinematheque.ca; 1131 Howe St, Downtown; tickets $12, double bills $16; 🚇10) This beloved cinema operates like an ongoing film festival with a daily-changing program of movies. A $3 annual membership is required – organize it at the door – before you can skulk in the dark with other chin-stroking movie buffs who probably named their children (or pets) after Fellini and Bergman.

Vancouver Whitecaps
SOCCER

(Map p48; ☎604-669-9283; www.whitecapsfc.com; 777 Pacific Blvd, BC Place Stadium, Yaletown; tickets from $45; ⊙Mar-Oct; ♿; S Stadium-Chinatown) Using BC Place Stadium (p50) as its home, Vancouver's professional soccer team plays in North America's top-tier Major League Soccer (MLS). Their on-field fortunes have ebbed and flowed since being promoted to the league in 2011, but they've

been finding their feet (useful for soccer players) lately. Make time to buy a souvenir soccer shirt to impress everyone back home.

Fresh Air Cinema
OUTDOOR CINEMA

(www.freshaircinema.ca; ♿) **FREE** Screening outdoor, admission-free movies at venues around Metro Vancouver every summer, the company's Stanley Park events often draw thousands of blanket-hugging locals. Check ahead to see what's on during your visit.

Vancouver Canucks
HOCKEY

(Map p48; ☎604-899-7400; www.nhl.com/canucks; 800 Griffiths Way, Rogers Arena, Downtown; tickets from $47; ⊙Sep-Apr; S Stadium-Chinatown) Recent years haven't been hugely successful for Vancouver's National Hockey League (NHL) team, which means it's sometimes easy to snag tickets to a game if you're simply visiting and want to see what 'ice hockey' (no one calls it that here) is all about. You'll hear 'go Canucks, go!' booming from the seats and in local bars on game nights.

🛍 Shopping

Vancouver's retail scene developed dramatically before the pandemic. Hit Robson St's mainstream chains, then discover the hip, independent shops of Gastown, Main St and Commercial Dr. Granville Island is stuffed with artsy stores and studios, while South Granville and Kitsilano's 4th Ave serve up a wide range of tempting boutiques.

★ Pacific Arts Market
ARTS & CRAFTS

(Map p46; ☎778-877-6449; www.pacificartsmarket.ca; 1448 W Broadway, South Granville; ⊙noon-5:30pm Tue & Wed, noon-7pm Thu & Fri, 11am-7pm Sat, 1-5pm Sun; 🚇9) Head upstairs to this large, under-the-radar gallery space and you'll find a kaleidoscopic array of stands showcasing the work of 40+ Vancouver and BC artists. From paintings to jewelry and from fiber arts to handmade chocolate bars, it's the perfect spot to find authentic souvenirs to take back home. The artists change regularly and there's something for every budget here.

★ Regional Assembly of Text
ARTS & CRAFTS

(Map p46; ☎604-877-2247; www.assemblyoftext.com; 3934 Main St; ⊙11am-6pm Mon-Sat, noon-5pm Sun; 🚇3) This ironic antidote to the digital age lures ink-stained locals with its journals, handmade pencil boxes and T-shirts printed with typewriter motifs. Check out the tiny under-the-stairs gallery showcasing global zines and don't miss the monthly Letter Writing Club (7pm, first Thursday of every month), where you can hammer on vintage typewriters, crafting erudite missives to faraway loved ones.

★ Paper Hound BOOKS

(Map p48; ☑604-428-1344; www.paperhound.ca; 344 W Pender St, Downtown; ⊙10am-7pm Sun-Thu, to 8pm Fri & Sat; ☐14) Proving the printed word is alive and kicking, this small but perfectly curated secondhand bookstore is a dog-eared favorite among locals. A perfect spot for browsing, you'll find tempting tomes (mostly used but some new) on everything from nature to poetry to chaos theory. Ask for recommendations; they really know their stuff here. Don't miss the bargain rack out front.

★ Red Cat Records MUSIC

(Map p46; ☑604-708-9422; www.redcat.ca; 4332 Main St; ⊙11am-7pm Mon-Thu, to 8pm Fri & Sat, to 6pm Sun; ☐3) Arguably Vancouver's coolest record store and certainly the only one named after a much-missed cat... There's a brilliantly curated collection of new and used vinyl and CDs, and it's co-owned by musicians; ask them for tips on where to see great local acts such as Loscil and Nick Krgovich or peruse the huge list of shows in the window.

★ Kitsilano Farmers Market MARKET

(Map p46; www.eatlocal.org; 2690 Larch St, Kitsilano Community Centre, Kitsilano; ⊙10am-2pm Sun May-Oct; ☐9) ✐ This seasonal farmers market is one of the city's most popular and is Kitsilano's best excuse to get out and hang with the locals. Arrive early for the best selection and you'll have the pick of freshly plucked local fruit and veg, such as sweet strawberries or spectacularly flavorful heirloom tomatoes. You'll likely never want to shop in a mainstream supermarket again.

Save some tummy room for the baked treats and peruse the arts and crafts; there may be something here of the handmade variety that will serve as a perfect souvenir of your West Coast visit.

★ Eastside Flea MARKET

(Map p46; www.eastsideflea.com; 550 Malkin Ave, Eastside Studios; $3-5; ⊙11am-5pm Sat & Sun, once or twice a month; ☐22) A size upgrade from its previous venue has delivered a cavernous market hall of hip arts and crafts-isans hawking everything from handmade chocolate bars to intricate jewelry and a humungous array of cool-ass vintage clothing. Give yourself plenty of time to hang out here; there's a pool table and retro arcade machines plus food trucks and a long bar serving local craft beer.

★ Karen Cooper Gallery ART

(Map p48; ☑604-559-5112; www.karencooper gallery.com; 1506 Duranleau St, Granville Island; ⊙10am-6pm, reduced hours in winter; ☐50) You'll feel like you've entered a tranquil forest clearing when you open the door of this delightful nature-themed photography gallery. Cooper's striking work focuses on BC's jaw-dropping wild beauty, from coniferous trees to grizzly bears. Take your time and don't be surprised if you fall in love with a handsome image of a bald eagle perched on a mountain tree.

ℹ Information

MEDICAL SERVICES

Shoppers Drug Mart (☑604-669-2424; 1125 Davie St, West End; ⊙24hr; ☐6) Pharmacy chain.

Ultima Medicentre (☑604-683-8138; 1055 Dunsmuir St, Downtown; ⊙8am-5pm Mon-Fri; Ⓢ Burrard) Full range of walk-in clinic medical services. Appointments not essential.

Vancouver General Hospital (☑604-875-4111; www.vch.ca; 855 W 12th Ave, Fairview; Ⓜ Broadway-City Hall)

MONEY

Vancouver Bullion & Currency Exchange (☑604-685-1008; www.vbce.ca; 800 W Pender St, Downtown; ⊙8:30am-5pm Mon-Fri; Ⓢ Granville) Aside from the banks, try Vancouver Bullion & Currency Exchange for currency exchange. It often has a wider range of currencies and competitive rates.

TOURIST INFORMATION

Tourism Vancouver Visitor Centre (☑604-683-2000; www.tourismvancouver.com; 200 Burrard St, Downtown; ⊙9am-5pm; Ⓢ Waterfront) A large repository of resources for visitors, with a staff of helpful advisers ready to assist in planning your trip in the city and around the area. Services and info available include free maps, visitor guides, accommodation and tour bookings, plus a host of glossy brochures on the city and the wider BC region.

ℹ Getting There & Away

If you've rented a car in the US and are driving it into Canada, bring a copy of the rental agreement to save any possible hassles with border officials.

Gas is generally cheaper in the US, so be sure to fill up before you cross into Canada.

STRETCH YOUR LEGS
VANCOUVER

Start/Finish: Gastown

Distance: 10km

Duration: Three to four hours

Wandering around Vancouver, with its visually arresting backdrop of sparkling ocean and snow-dusted mountaintops, you discover there's more to this city than appearances. It's a kaleidoscope of distinctive neighborhoods, strongly artistic and just as hip as it is sophisticated.

GASTOWN

Crammed into a dozen, often brick-paved blocks, trendy Gastown is where the city began. Century-old heritage buildings now house cool bars and quirky galleries, with the landmark **steam clock** (cnr Water & Cambie Sts; ⑤ Waterfront) whistling to a camera-wielding coterie of onlookers every 15 minutes. Tucked along handsome historic rows, swish boutiques, artisan stores and chatty coffee shops invite leisurely browsing and laid-back java sipping. And when you need a fuel-up, **Brioche** (www.brioche.ca; 401 W Cordova St; mains $10-16; ⊘ 7am-9pm Mon-Fri, 8am-9pm Sat & Sun; ⑤ Waterfront) is a colorful, comfy place to stop for lunch.

The Walk ⟫ Follow Water St east, turning right on Carrall St and heading south for three blocks to Pender St and Chinatown.

CHINATOWN

North America's third-largest Chinatown is a highly wanderable explosion of sight, sound and aromas. Check out the towering **Chinatown Millennium Gate** (cnr W Pender & Taylor Sts; ⑤ Stadium-Chinatown) and visit the tranquil **Dr Sun Yat-Sen Classical Chinese Garden** (www.vancouverchinesegarden.com; 578 Carrall St; adult/child $14/10; ⊘ 9:30am-7pm mid-Jun–Aug, 10am-6pm Sep & May–mid-Jun, 10am-4:30pm Oct-Apr; ⑤ Stadium-Chinatown). Save time for the **Chinese Tea Shop** (www.thechineseteashop.com; 101 E Pender St; ⊘ 1-6pm Wed-Mon; ▣ 3), which has all the makings of a perfect cuppa, and slip into colorful apothecary stores for a fascinating eyeful of traditional Chinese medicine.

The Walk ⟫ Follow Keefer St and Keefer Pl west, crossing the roundabout at the end and continuing along the footpath to Beatty St. Turn left and walk three blocks to Robson St. Turn right, crossing Granville St, and continue along Robson to Hornby St.

VANCOUVER ART GALLERY

A palatial former courthouse building, the grand home of the **Vancouver Art Gallery** (www.vanartgallery.bc.ca; 750 Hornby St, Downtown; adult/child $24/6.50; ⊘ 10am-5pm Wed-Mon, to 9pm Tue; ▣ 5) showcas-

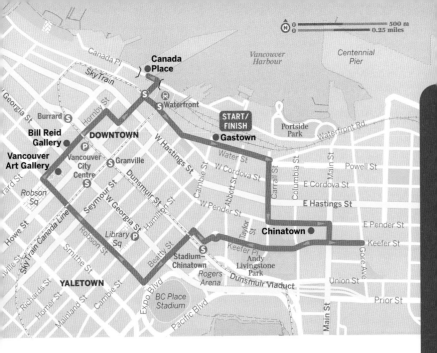

es contemporary exhibitions, work by time-honored masters, and blockbuster international traveling shows. Check out FUSE (www.vanartgallery.bc.ca/fuse; $29; ☺8pm-midnight), a regular late-night party event where you can hang out with the city's young creatives over wine and live music. Check ahead for regular gallery talks and tours and, if you're traveling on a tight budget, consider postponing your visit to a Tuesday when entry is by donation after 5pm.

The Walk ≫ Exit the gallery on the Hornby St side and walk two blocks northeast along Hornby.

BILL REID GALLERY

The Bill Reid Gallery of Northwest Coast Art (www.billreidgallery.ca; 639 Hornby St, Downtown; adult/youth/child $13/6/free; ☺10am-5pm May-Sep, 11am-5pm Wed-Sun Oct-Apr; ⑤Burrard) showcases carvings, paintings and jewelry from Canada's most revered Haida artist as well as his fellow First Nations creators. This is one of the city's must-visit art galleries if you're interested in the region's rich First Nations

heritage. Give yourself plenty of time for a full-on cultural immersion here.

The Walk ≫ Continue up Hornby St to Pender St. Turn right and then left onto Howe St. Follow this towards the water.

CANADA PLACE

Shaped like a series of sails jutting into the sky over the harbor, Canada Place (www.canadaplace.ca; 999 Canada Place Way, Downtown; ⑫ ♿; ⑤Waterfront) is a cruise-ship terminal, convention center and pier where you can stroll the waterfront and enjoy handsome views of the grand North Shore mountains. Save time to snap photos of the floatplanes landing and taking off alongside, framed by Stanley Park in the background. Next door, check out the grass-roofed convention-center expansion and the tripod-like Olympic Cauldron, a permanent reminder of the 2010 Games.

The Walk ≫ Backtrack up Howe St for one block and turn left onto W Cordova St. After three blocks, edge left onto Water St and back into Gastown.

THE KOOTENAYS & THE ROCKIES

You can't help sighing as you ponder the plethora of snow-covered peaks in BC's Kootenay region. Deep river valleys cleaved by white-water rivers, impossibly sheer rock faces, alpine meadows and a sawtooth of white-dappled mountains stretching across the horizon inspire awe, action and contemplation.

Coming from the west, the mountain majesty builds as if choreographed. The roughly parallel ranges of the Monashees and the Selkirks striate the West Kootenays, with the Arrow Lakes adding texture. Appealing towns such as Revelstoke and Nelson nestle against the mountains and are outdoor fun centers year-round. The East Kootenays cover the Purcell Mountains region below Golden, taking in Radium Hot Springs and delightful Fernie.

BC's Rocky Mountains national parks (Mt Revelstoke, Glacier, Yoho and Kootenay) don't have the profile of Banff and Jasper over the border, but for many that's an advantage: each has its own spectacular qualities, often relatively unexploited by Banff-bound hordes.

Revelstoke

☑ 250, 778 / POP 7950

Laden with history, this picturesque mountain gateway has a lot going for it. The local arts community is thriving and there are abundant opportunities for hiking, kayaking and, best of all, skiing.

It's more than worth a long pause as you pass on Hwy 1, which bypasses the town center to the northeast. The main streets include 1st St and Mackenzie Ave.

◎ Sights

Grizzly Plaza, between Mackenzie and Orton Aves, is a pedestrian precinct and the heart of downtown, where free live-music performances take place every evening in July and August.

While outdoor activities are Revelstoke's real drawcard, a stroll of the center and a moment spent at the museums is a must. Pick up the *Public Art* and *Heritage* walking-tour brochures at the visitor center (p64).

★**Mt Revelstoke National Park**　　　PARK
(www.pc.gc.ca/revelstoke; off Hwy 1; adult/child incl Glacier National Park $7.80/free) Grand in beauty if not in size, this 260-sq-km national park, just northeast of its namesake town, is a vision of peaks and valleys – many all but untrodden.

NICK FITZHARDINGE/GETTY IMAGES ©

Mt Revelstoke National Park

There are several good hiking trails from the summit. To overnight in the wild, you must have a Wilderness Pass camping permit ($10, in addition to your park pass), available from **Parks Canada Revelstoke Office** (☑250-837-7500; www.pc.gc.ca; 301 3rd St; ☉8am-4:30pm Mon-Fri) or Rogers Pass Centre (p64) inside Glacier National Park (p64).

★ **Jones Distilling** DISTILLERY
(www.jonesdistilling.com; 616 3 St W; ☉noon-6pm Thu-Sun) In what was the 1914-built brick Mountain View School building, over the road from the Columbia River, Jones Distillery is making a name with its award-winning Revelstoke Gin Series and Mr Jones Vodka. Focusing on local ingredients and Revelstoke enthusiasm, the rewards are coming. Book tastings and tours through the Canadian Gin Guild (www.canadianginguild.com).

Revelstoke Railway Museum MUSEUM
(☑250-837-6060; www.railwaymuseum.com; 719 Track St W; adult/child $10/5; ☉9am-5pm May-Sep, shorter hours Oct-Apr; ℙ) In an attractive building across the tracks from the town center, this museum contains restored steam locomotives, including one of the largest steam engines ever used on Canadian Pacific Railway (CPR) lines. Photographs and artifacts document the construction of the CPR, which was instrumental – actually, essential – in linking eastern and western Canada.

🏃 Activities

Sandwiched between the vast but relatively unknown Selkirk and Monashee mountain ranges, Revelstoke draws serious snow buffs looking for vast landscapes of crowd-free powder. It's where North America's first ski jump was built, in 1915.

For cross-country skiing, head to the 22km of groomed trails at Mt MacPherson Ski Area, 7km south of town on Hwy 23; see www.revelstokenordic.org for information.

All that white snow turns into white water come spring and rafting is big here. Mountain biking is also huge; pick up trail maps from the visitor center (p64).

Revelstoke Mountain Resort SKIING
(☑866-373-4754; www.revelstokemountainresort. com; Camozzi Rd; 1-day lift ticket adult/child $88/30) Just 6km southeast of town, the Revelstoke Mountain Resort has ambitions to become the biggest ski resort this side of the Alps. It has seemingly endless virgin slopes and 65

❶ AVALANCHE WARNING

The Kootenays are the heart of avalanche country. Such events kill more people in BC each year than any other natural phenomenon – the annual toll is stubbornly high.

Avalanches can occur at any time, even on terrain that seems relatively flat. Roughly half the people caught in one don't survive. It's vital that people venturing out onto the snow ask about conditions first; if an area is closed, don't go there. Whether you're backcountry ski touring or simply hiking in the alpine region, you'll want to rent a homing beacon; most outdoors shops can supply one.

In Revelstoke, **Avalanche Canada** (☑250-837-2141; www.avalanche.ca) tracks avalanche reports and offers forecasts for BC and the Canadian Rockies. It has a vital website and a phone app.

runs. In one run you can ski both 700m of bowl and 700m of trees. At 1713m, the vertical drop is the greatest in North America.

Apex Rafting Co RAFTING
(☑250-837-6376; www.apexrafting.com; 112 1st St E; adult/child $124/99; ☉Jun-Aug; ﹪) Runs kid-friendly two-hour guided trips on the Illecillewaet River in spring and summer.

Wandering Wheels CYCLING
(☑250-814-7609; www.wanderingwheels.ca; 120 MacKenzie Ave; lessons per hour from $35, tours from $60; ☉Jun-Oct) Offers bike shuttle services, lessons, heli-bike and tours.

🛏 Sleeping

★ **Regent Hotel** HOTEL **$$**
(☑250-837-2107; www.regenthotel.ca; 112 1st St E; r from $110; ℙ☕❄🛜🛁) The poshest place in the center is not lavish, but it is comfy. The 42 modern rooms bear no traces of the hotel's 1914 roots and exterior. The restaurant and lounge are justifiably popular. Many guests bob the night away in the outdoor hot tub.

Swiss Chalet Motel MOTEL **$$**
(☑877-837-4650; www.swisschaletmotel.com; 1101 West Victoria Rd; r from $96; ℙ☕❄🛜) Rooms may be small, but they're clean and comfy at this place on the main road, a 10-minute walk from the center of Revelstoke. Perks

include a complimentary breakfast, tickets to the aquatic center, guest laundry and a free shuttle service during ski season to Revelstoke Mountain Resort (p63).

Courthouse Inn
B&B $$

(☑250-837-3369; www.courthouseinnrevelstoke. com; 312 Kootenay St; r from $129; P ⊕ ❄ 🛜) A quiet 10-room B&B close to the center. Extras include a lavish breakfast, boot and glove driers for winter and lots of personal service. Rooms have no TV or phone.

✕ Eating & Drinking

★ Modern Bakeshop & Café
CAFE $

(☑250-837-6886; www.themodernbakeshopand cafe.com; 212 Mackenzie Ave; mains from $6; ⊙6:30am-5pm Mon-Sat; 🛜) Try a croque monsieur (grilled ham-and-cheese sandwich) or an elaborate pastry for a taste of Europe at this cute art-deco cafe. Many items, such as the muffins, are made with organic ingredients. Discover the baked 'boofy uptrack bar' for a treat. Nice seating outside.

Taco Club
MEXICAN $

(☑250-837-0988; www.thetacoclub.ca; 206 Mackenzie Ave; mains from $6; ⊙11am-10pm) Once Revelstoke's favorite food truck, Taco Club has now laid down some roots in a vintage building downtown. Tacos and burritos are excellent, and all the usual suspects for sides are available. Enjoy the outside seating on long summer evenings.

Old School Eatery
CANADIAN $$

(☑250-814-4144; www.oldschooleatery.ca; 616 3 St W; dinner mains from $14; ⊙11am-9pm Tue-Fri, from 9am Sat & Sun) Sharing the old Mountain View School building of 1914 with Jones Distilling (p63), the Old School Eatery is becoming a favorite in Revelstoke, particularly for brunch in the weekends. With what they describe as 'sophisticated comfort food', you'll find top dinner options too, such as Creole pork chop ($28) and Moroccan lamb chops ($32), all in an old school room.

★ Mt Begbie Brewing
MICROBREWERY

(☑250-837-2756; www.mt-begbie.com; 2155 Oak Dr; ⊙11:30am-9pm Mon-Sat, tours at 4pm) Head out just east of town to Mt Begbie's tasting area and store to try the popular local brews. The Powerhouse Pale Ale and the Brave Liver, a seasonal winter Scottish pale ale (at 6.5%), should put a smile on your face. There's decent food plus both indoor and outdoor seating.

❶ Information

Revelstoke Visitor Center (☑250-837-5345; www.seerevelstoke.com; 301 Victoria Rd; ⊙8:30am-7pm) Excellent source for hiking and mountain-biking info and maps.

❶ Getting There & Away

Riders Express (www.riderexpress.ca) runs buses connecting Vancouver, Kamloops and Calgary, with a bus stopping daily in Revelstoke and Golden in both directions.

Revelstoke to Golden

Keep your eyes on the road or, better yet, let someone else drive as you traverse the Trans-Canada Hwy (Hwy 1) for 148km between Revelstoke and Golden. Stunning mountain peaks follow one after another as you go.

Glacier National Park
PARK

(www.pc.gc.ca; adult/child incl Mt Revelstoke National Park $8/4) To be accurate, this 1350-sq-km park should be called '430 Glaciers National Park'. The annual snowfall can be as much as 23m, and due to the sheer mountain slopes, this is one of the world's most active avalanche areas. For this reason, skiing, caving and mountaineering are regulated; you must register with park wardens before venturing into the backcountry. Check the weather and get an avalanche report (p63). Rogers Pass ranks as one of the world's most beautiful mountain passes.

Be sure to pause at the Hemlock Grove Trail, 54km east of Revelstoke, where a 400m boardwalk winds through an ancient hemlock rainforest.

Glacier National Park has good camping options at Illecillewaet Campground (www.pc.gc.ca; Rogers Pass, off Hwy 1; tent & RV sites from $16; ⊙late Jun–early Oct) and Loop Brook Campground (www.pc.gc.ca; Rogers Pass, off Hwy 1; tent & RV sites from $16; ⊙ Jul–late Sep), both on the Revelstoke side of Rogers Pass. Sites are available on a first-come, first-served basis. Otherwise, you'll need to stay in either Revelstoke or Golden.

Rogers Pass Centre (☑250-814-5233; off Hwy 1; ⊙8am-7pm mid-Jun–early Sep, shorter hours mid-Sep–mid-Jun) displays Canadian Pacific Railway (CPR) dioramas, halfway between Revelstoke and Golden. It show films about Glacier National Park, organizes guided walks in summer and has an excellent bookstore run by the Friends of Mt Revelstoke and Glacier.

Golden

☑ 250, 778 / POP 3700

Golden is well situated for national-park explorations – there are six nearby. Whitewater rafting excitement lies even closer, where the Kicking Horse River converges with the Columbia.

⦿ Sights & Activities

Golden is the center for white-water rafting trips on the turbulent and chilly Kicking Horse River. Along with the powerful grade III and IV rapids, the breathtaking scenery along the sheer walls of the Kicking Horse Valley makes this rafting experience one of North America's best.

Northern Lights Wolf Centre PARK
(☑ 250-344-6798; www.northernlightswildlife.com; 1745 Short Rd; adult/child $12/6; ⊙ 9am-7pm Jul & Aug, 10am-6pm May, Jun & Sep, noon-5pm Oct-Apr; ℗) This small wildlife center houses a small pack of gray wolves and wolf-husky crosses, all born and bred in captivity. Visits include an introduction to the resident wolves – although most of the viewing is done through wire-frame pens.

★ Alpine Rafting RAFTING
(☑ 250-344-6521; www.alpinerafting.com; 1509 Lafontaine Rd; raft trips from $89; ⊙ Jun-Sep; 🚣) Offers several good family rafting options, including a white-water run for kids aged four years and over, right up to the more extreme class IV+ 'Kicking Horse Challenge.'

Kicking Horse Mountain Resort SKIING, MOUNTAIN BIKING
(☑ 250-439-5425; www.kickinghorseresort.com; Kicking Horse Trail; 1-day lift ticket adult/child winter $94/38, summer $42/21) With a 1260m (4133ft) vertical drop and a snowy position between the Rockies and the Purcells, the resort's popularity grows each year. After the expert-level ski slopes, it's renowned for summer mountain biking, which includes the longest cycling descent in Canada. The resort is 14km west of Golden, which can be seen year-round from the Golden Eye Gondola.

🛏 Sleeping

★ Dreamcatcher Hostel HOSTEL $
(☑ 250-439-1090; www.dreamcatcherhostel.com; 528 9th Ave N; dm/r from $32/90; ℗ ☕ 🛜) Run by two veteran travelers, this centrally located hostel has everything a budget traveler could hope for. There are three dorm rooms, five private rooms, as well as a vast kitchen and a comfy common room with a stone fireplace. Outside there's a garden and a barbecue.

Kicking Horse Canyon B&B GUESTHOUSE $$
(☑ 250-899-0840; www.kickinghorsecanyonbb.com; 644 Lapp Rd; d from $120; ℗ ☕ 🛜) Hidden away among the hills to the east of Golden, this endearingly offbeat B&B takes you into the family the minute you cross the threshold.

Glacier National Park

Run by genial host Jeannie Cook and her husband, Jerry, it's a real alpine home-away-from-home, surrounded by private grassy grounds with views across the mountains.

Chancellor Peak Chalets LODGE $$$

(📞250-344-7038; www.chancellorpeakchalets. com; 2924 Kicking Horse Rd; cabins from $289; P🐕❄🛜) The 11 log chalets at this riverside retreat have two levels and sleep up to six. There are soaker tubs, full kitchens and all the nature you can breathe in. The chalets are 25km southeast of Golden, just outside Yoho National Park.

✖ Eating & Drinking

★ Bacchus Books & Cafe CAFE $

(📞250-344-5600; www.bacchusbooks.ca; 409 9th Ave N; mains from $8; ⊙9am-5:30pm) This bohemian hideaway at the end of 8th St is a favorite haunt for Golden's artsy crowd. Browse for books (new and secondhand) in the downstairs bookstore, then head upstairs to find a table for tea among the higgledy-piggledy shelves. Sandwiches, salads and cakes are made on the premises, and the coffee is as good as you'll find in Golden.

★ Island Restaurant INTERNATIONAL $$

(📞250-344-2400; www.islandrestaurant.ca; 101 10th Ave; dinner mains from $14; ⊙9am-9pm) On a small river island in the middle of Kicking Horse River in the center of Golden, this place features a flower-embellished riverside patio and international dishes and drinks. The food wears many hats, from a Jamaican-jerk chicken sandwich to Thai Thursdays and full-on Mexican nights on Mondays and Tuesdays.

Wolf Den PUB FOOD $$

(📞250-344-9863; www.thewolfsdengolden.ca; 1105 9th St; dinner mains from $14; ⊙4-10pm) An excellent pub with live music on Sundays. It's hugely popular with locals, who love the burgers and hearty fare, which are way above average. The beer menu includes some of BC's best on tap. It's just south of the river from downtown.

★ Whitetooth Brewing MICROBREWERY

(📞250-344-2838; www.whitetoothbrewing.com; 623 8th Ave N; ⊙2-10pm) Golden's microbrewery features tank-to-tap brews and a marvelous sunny patio for those long summer evenings. Whitetooth is a hit with locals who come to fill their growlers and relax on the patio. We like the Icefields Belgian-inspired pale ale.

ℹ Information

Golden Visitor Information Centre (📞250-439-7290; www.tourismgolden.com; 1000 Hwy 1; ⊙9am-7pm Jun-Sep) In a purpose-built building on Hwy 1 and Hwy 95 into town from the southeast.

ℹ Getting There & Away

Riders Express (www.riderexpress.ca) Runs buses connecting Vancouver, Kamloops and Calgary, with a bus stopping daily in Revelstoke and Golden in both directions.

Yoho National Park

The surging waters of glacier-fed, ice-blue Kicking Horse River that plow through a valley of the same name are an apt image for dramatic Yoho National Park. This spectacular park is home to looming peaks, pounding waterfalls, glacial lakes and patches of pretty meadows.

⊙ Sights & Activities

★ Yoho National Park NATIONAL PARK

(📞250-343-6783; www.pc.gc.ca; off Hwy 1; adult/child $10/5) Although the smallest (1310 sq km) of the four national parks in the Rockies, Yoho is a diamond in the (very) rough. This wilderness is the real deal; it's some of the continent's least tarnished.

East of Field on Hwy 1 is the Takakkaw Falls road, open from late June to early October. At 255m, Takakkaw Falls (p67) is one of the highest waterfalls in Canada. From here the Iceline Trail, a 20km hiking loop, passes many glaciers and spectacular scenery.

Near the south gate of the park, you can reach pretty Wapta Falls along a 2.4km trail. The easy walk takes about 45 minutes each way.

Don't miss the surging waters at Natural Bridge, which you can admire on the short drive from Hwy 1 near Field to iconic Emerald Lake (p67).

★ Burgess Shale Fossil Beds NATIONAL PARK

This World Heritage site protects the amazing Cambrian-age fossil beds on Mt Stephen and Mt Field. These 515-million-year-old fossils preserve the remains of marine creatures that were some of the earliest forms of life on earth. You can only get to the fossil beds by guided hikes, which are led by naturalists from the Burgess Shale Geoscience Foundation (p68). Reservations are essential.

Kicking Horse Pass & Spiral Tunnels
VIEWPOINT

The historic Kicking Horse Pass between Banff and Yoho National Parks is one of the most important passes in the Canadian Rockies. It was discovered in 1858 by the Palliser Expedition, which was tasked with discovering a possible route across the Rockies for the Canadian Pacific Railway. Accessible 8km east of Field from the westbound lanes of Hwy 1, the viewing area is often closed and the view obscured by vegetation.

Takakkaw Falls
WATERFALL

A thundering torrent of water tumbles from its source in the nearby Daly Glacier over a sheer cliff face for 255m (836ft), making it the second-highest waterfall in Canada. At the end of the road, a trail leads for around 800m (half a mile) from the Takakkaw parking lot to the base of the falls. The road is open from late June to early October.

Emerald Lake
LAKE

For most visitors, this vividly colored lake is Yoho's most unmissable sight. Ringed by forest and silhouetted by impressive mountains, including the iconic profile of **Mt Burgess** to the southeast, it's a truly beautiful – if incredibly busy – spot. Escape the mobs in a rental canoe. The lake road is signed off Hwy 1 just to the southwest of Field and continues for 10km (6.2 miles) to the lake shore.

🛏 Sleeping

The campgrounds within Yoho close from mid-October to mid-May. In addition to a couple of lodges in the park, you can find a range of lodgings in Field.

Kicking Horse Campground
CAMPGROUND $

(www.reservation.pc.gc.ca; Yoho Valley Rd; tent & RV sites $27.40; ⊗May 23–Oct 14; P🐾) This is probably the most popular campground in Yoho. It's in a nice forested location, with plenty of space between the 88 sites, and there are showers. Riverside sites (especially 68 to 74) are the pick of the bunch.

HI-Yoho National Park
HOSTEL $

(Whiskey Jack Hostel; ☎403-670-7580; www.hihostels.ca; Yoho Valley Rd; dm from $28; ⊗Jun 29–Sep 23) Yoho National Park's Takakkaw Falls are so close you can see them from the hostel's timber deck. Three nine-bed dorms and a basic kitchen comprise the rudimentary facilities; it's usually booked out in summer.

Lake O'Hara

Perched high in the mountains, Lake O'Hara is an encapsulation of the Rockies region, and worth the significant hassle to reach it. Compact wooded hillsides, alpine meadows, snow-covered passes, mountain vistas and glaciers wrap around the stunning lake. A day trip is rewarding, but if you stay overnight in the backcountry you'll be able to

Hiking the Iceline Trail, Yoho National Park

access many hiking trails – some quite difficult, and all quite spectacular. The Alpine Circuit (12km) has a bit of everything.

Lake O'Hara Campground
CAMPGROUND **$**

(🖉 reservations 250-343-6433; www.pc.gc.ca; Yoho National Park; tent sites $10, reservation fee $12; ⊙ mid-Jun–Sep) Reserve three months in advance to snare one of 30 campsites. Available spots are often taken in the first hour that reservation phone lines are open (from 8am Mountain time). If you don't have advance reservations, three to five campsites are set aside for 'standby' users; call at 8am the day before you wish to stay.

★ Lake O'Hara Lodge
LODGE **$$$**

(🖉 250-343-6418; www.lakeohara.com; Yoho National Park; s/d from $500/665, cabins $940; ⊙ Jan-Apr & Jun-Oct; 🖨 🛜) 🖉 Leaving guests slack-jawed for more than 90 years, the lodge is the only place to stay at the lake if you're not traveling with a tent. It's luxurious in a rustic way, and its environmental practices are lauded. Food comes from BC producers and is excellent. Minimum stay is two nights.

ⓘ Getting There & Away

To reach the lake, take the **shuttle bus** (🖉 reservations 877-737-3783; www.pc.gc.ca; adult/child return $15/8, reservation fee $12; ⊙ mid-Jun–Sep) from the Lake O'Hara parking lot, 15km east of Field on Hwy 1. A quota system governs bus access to the lake. Given the lake's popularity, reservations are basically mandatory, unless you want to walk. That said, if you don't have advance reservations, six day-use seats on the bus are set aside for 'standby' users. Call at 8am the day before and think 'lucky.'

You can freely walk the 11km from the parking area, but no bikes are allowed. The area around Lake O'Hara usually remains covered with snow or else stays very muddy until mid-July.

Field

Right off Hwy 1, this historic railroad town is worth a stop for its dramatic overlook of the river and quaint yet unfussy atmosphere. Many buildings date from the early days of the railways, when the town was the Canadian Pacific Railway's headquarters for exploration and, later, for strategic planning, when engineers were working on the problem of moving trains over Kicking Horse Pass.

Burgess Shale
Geoscience Foundation
HIKING

(🖉 800-343-3006; www.burgess-shale.bc.ca; 201 Kicking Horse Ave; tours adult/child from $94.50/65; ⊙ 9am-4pm Tue-Sat mid-Jun–mid-Sep) The only way to visit the amazing 515-million-year-old Burgess Shale fossil beds (p66) is on a hike led by the Burgess Shale Geoscience Foundation. Book online and follow instructions for the morning meeting location. There are two core hikes, one to Walcott Quarry and another to the adjacent fossil fields on Mt Stephen.

Both are strenuous full-day trips with plenty of elevation gain, so you'll need to be fit and wear proper footwear.

★ Truffle Pigs Lodge
HOTEL **$$**

(🖉 250-343-6303; www.trufflepigs.com; 100 Centre St; r from $120; ⊙ Jun-Sep; P 🖨 ❄ 🛜) Field's only hotel is a timber building with heritage charm. The 14 rooms are fairly simply decked out, though. Some have small kitchens. The owners run the town's well-known restaurant, Truffle Pigs bistro (mains from $12; ⊙ 8am-9pm; 🛜) 🖉, in the same attractive building.

ⓘ Information

Yoho National Park Information Centre

(🖉 250-343-6783; www.pc.gc.ca; off Hwy 1; ⊙ 9am-7pm May-Oct) Pick up maps and trail descriptions. Rangers can advise on itineraries and conditions. Alberta Tourism staffs a desk here in summer and Friends of Yoho maintains a book shop.

Alpine Circuit, Lake O'Hara
JAMES HAGUE/SHUTTERSTOCK ©

Kootenay National Park

Kootenay is the the only national park in Canada with both glaciers and cacti. From Radium Hot Springs you can create a fine driving loop through Kootenay into Alberta's Banff National Park, then back into BC at Golden through Yoho National Park; many of the top sights are easily reached by car.

The very remote Mt Assiniboine Provincial Park (p69) offers true adventurers a remarkable wilderness experience.

⊙ Sights

Kootenay National Park   NATIONAL PARK
(☑ 250-347-9505; www.pc.gc.ca/kootenay; Hwy 93; adult/child $9.80/free, tent/RV sites $21.50/38.20; ⊙ camping May-Oct) Shaped like a lightning bolt, 1406-sq-km Kootenay National Park is centered on a long, wide, tree-covered valley shadowed by cold, gray peaks. It has a more moderate climate than other Rocky Mountains parks and, in the southern regions especially, summers can be hot and dry, which is a factor in the frequent fires.

The interpretive Fireweed Trails (500m or 2km) loop through the surrounding forest at the north end of Hwy 93. Panels explain how nature is recovering from a 1968 fire. Some 7km further on, Marble Canyon (p19) has a pounding creek flowing through a nascent forest. Another 3km south on the main road you'll find the easy 2km trail through forest to ocher pools known as the Paint Pots. Panels describe both the mining history of this rusty earth and its importance to Indigenous people.

Learn how the park's appearance has changed over time at the Kootenay Valley Viewpoint, where informative panels vie with the view. Just 3km south, Olive Lake makes a perfect picnic or rest stop. A 500m lakeside interpretive trail describes some of the visitors who've come before you.

Mt Assiniboine Provincial Park   PARK
(www.env.gov.bc.ca/bcparks) Between Kootenay and Banff National Parks lies this lesser-known and smaller (39-sq-km) provincial park, part of the Rockies' Unesco World Heritage site. The pointed peak of Mt Assiniboine (3618m), often referred to as Canada's Matterhorn, and its near neighbors have become a magnet for experienced rock climbers and mountaineers. Backcountry hikers revel in its meadows and glaciers.

The park's main focus is crystal-clear Lake Magog, which is reachable on a 27km trek from Banff National Park or by helicopter. At the lake, there's a lodge, camping and huts.

🛏 Sleeping

Kootenay National Park has a few lodges and campgrounds inside its border, and nearby Radium Hot Springs has a huge number of lodgings. Mt Assiniboine Provincial Park is limited to wilderness camping, a few huts and a remote lodge.

★ Kootenay Park Lodge   CABIN $$
(☑ 403-762-9196; www.kootenayparklodge.com; Hwy 93, Vermilion Crossing, Kootenay National Park; d cabins from $125; ⊙ mid-May–late Sep; 🅿 😊 📶) The pick of the few places to stay inside the park, this lodge has a range of cute log cabins complete with verandah, fridge and hot plates. Think rustic charm. There is a restaurant open June 1 through mid-September, a general store selling coffee and snacks, and for those who can't do without it, spotty wi-fi.

Assiniboine Lodge   LODGE $$$
(☑ 403-678-2883; www.assiniboinelodge.com; Mt Assiniboine Provincial Park; r per person $350, shared & private cabin per person from $350; ⊙ Feb, Mar & Jun-Oct; 📶) The only lodge in Assiniboine is also the oldest ski lodge in the Canadian Rockies, surrounded by mountain meadows and gloriously backed by Mt Assiniboine. Rustic rooms sleep one or two people (solo travelers usually must share), plus there are shared (three to five people) or private cabins. Rates include meals and hiking-guide service. Helicopter transport is $175 each way.

ℹ Information

The main **Kootenay National Park visitor center** (☑ 250-347-9331; www.radiumhot-springs.com; 7556 Main St E; ⊙ visitor center 9am-5pm year-round, Parks Canada May-Oct, later in summer; 📶) is in Radium Hot Springs. It has excellent resources for hikers.

ℹ CHECK YOUR WATCH

It is a constant source of confusion that the East Kootenays lie in the Mountain time zone, along with Alberta, unlike the rest of BC, which falls within the Pacific time zone. West on Hwy 1 from Golden, the time changes at the east gate of Glacier National Park. Going west on Hwy 3, the time changes between Cranbrook and Creston. Mountain time is one hour later than Pacific time.

Radium Hot Springs

Cornered in the southwest of Kootenay National Park, Radium Hot Springs is a major jumping off point for the entire Rocky Mountains national park area.

Radium boasts a large resident population of bighorn sheep, which often wander through town, but the big attraction is the namesake hot springs, 3km northeast of town.

There's a definite German-Austrian vibe here with accommodations such as Motel Tyrol, Alpen Motel, Motel Bavaria, restaurants like the Old Salzburg and Helna Stube, and even an Edelweiss St.

Radium Hot Springs   HOT SPRINGS
(☑ 250-347-9485; www.pc.gc.ca/hotsprings; off Hwy 93; adult/child $7.30/4.95; ☉ 9am-11pm) The large hot springs pools have just been modernized and can get very busy in summer. The water comes from the ground at 44°C, enters the first pool at 39°C and hits the cooler one at 29°C. It's 3km northeast of the township, inside the park gate, with plenty of parking.

Radium Park Lodge   MOTEL $
(☑ 778-527-4857; www.radiumparklodge.com; 4873 Stanley St; r from $79; P ⊜ ✳ 🛜 ☒) Clean and comfortable motel rooms at Radium Hot Springs, near the entrance to the parks. Continental breakfast is included and there's plenty of parking a couple of blocks back from the highway.

Inn on Canyon   GUESTHOUSE $$
(☑ 250-347-9392; www.villagecountryinn.bc.ca; 7557 Canyon Ave; r from $109; P ⊜ 🛜) A cute gabled house just off the main drag. Its rooms are sparkling clean and decked out in country fashion.

BC MASCOTS
Some BC towns have their own quirky mascots, which sometimes appear at community events. On your travels, look out for **Knuckles** the grey whale in Ucluelet; **Peter Pine** the tree in Princeton; **Mr PG** in Prince George; and, our favorite, **Potato Jack** in Pemberton – a jaunty tuber dressed as a cowboy, complete with spurs and a neckerchief.

Big Horn Cafe   CAFE $
(☑ 403-861-2972; www.bighorncafe.net; 7527 Main St; snacks from $3; ☉ 6am-4:30pm; 🛜) An ideal road-trip breaker where you can refuel with coffee and a cinnamon bun or something more savory.

Radium Hot Springs to Fernie

South from Radium Hot Springs, Hwy 93/95 follows the wide Columbia River valley between the Purcell and Rocky Mountains. It's not especially interesting, unless you're into the area's industry (ski-resort construction), agriculture (golf courses) or wild game (condo buyers).

South of Skookumchuck on Hwy 93/95, the road forks. Go left on Hwy 95 and you'll come to Fort Steele Heritage Town (p28).

From Fort Steele, it's 95km to Fernie along Hwys 93 and 3.

Fernie
☑ 250 / POP 5250

Surrounded by mountains on four sides – that's the sheer granite Lizard Range you see looking west – Fernie defines cool. Once devoted solely to lumber and coal, the town has used its sensational setting to branch out. Skiers love the 8m-plus of dry powder that annually blankets the runs seen from town. In summer, this same dramatic setting lures scores of hikers and mountain bikers.

Despite the town's discovery by pleasure seekers, it still retains a down-to-earth, vintage-brick vibe, best felt in the cafes, bars, shops and galleries along Victoria (2nd) Ave in the historic center, three blocks south of Hwy 3 (7th Ave).

◉ Sights & Activities

Fernie Museum   MUSEUM
(☑ 250-423-7016; www.ferniemuseum.com; 491 2nd Ave; adult/child $5/free; ☉ 10am-5:30pm) Impressively housed in a 1909 bank building, the Fernie Museum has engaging displays and is an excellent source of info about the town and region. Experience the fires, floods, booms and busts that have shaped the town.

Mt Fernie Provincial Park   PARK
(☑ 250-422-3003; www.env.gov.bc.ca/bcparks; Mt Fernie Park Rd, off Hwy 3) Mountain biking is popular at Mt Fernie Provincial Park, just

3km south of town. It also offers hikes for all skills and interests, plus camping.

★ Fernie Alpine Resort — SKIING

(☎250-423-4655; www.skifernie.com; 5339 Ski Area Rd; 1-day pass adult/child $94/38) In fall, all eyes turn to the mountains for more than just their beauty: they're looking for snow. A five-minute drive from downtown, fast-growing Fernie Alpine Resort boasts 142 runs, five bowls and almost endless dumps of powder. Most hotels run shuttles here daily.

Guide's Hut — CYCLING

(☎250-423-3650; www.theguideshut.ca; 671 2 Ave; guiding per hour $30; ⏱10am-6pm) Raise your mountain-biking game with expert coaching and instruction, and let them show you the far reaches of the Elk Valley.

Mountain High River Adventures — RAFTING

(☎250-423-5008; www.raftfernie.com; 2001 6th Ave; trips adult/child from $140/100; ⏱8am-6pm May-Sep) The Elk River is a classic whitewater river, with three grade IV rapids and 11 grade III rapids. In addition to rafting, Mountain High offers kayaking, floats, rentals and more on the surging waters. Its Adventure Centre is at Fernie RV Resort.

🛏 Sleeping

HI Raging Elk Hostel — HOSTEL $

(☎250-423-6811; www.ragingelk.com; 892 6th Ave; dm/r from $30/85; 🅿🐕🀫) Wide decks allow plenty of inspirational mountain-gazing at this well-run central hostel. Raging Elk has good advice for those hoping to mix time on the slopes or trails with seasonal work. The pub (open 4pm to midnight) is a hoot (and offers cheap beer).

★ Park Place Lodge — HOTEL $$

(☎250-423-6871; www.parkplacelodge.com; 742 Hwy 3; r from $130; 🅿🐕❄🀫) The nicest lodging close to the center, Park Place offers 64 comfortable rooms with fridge and microwave, and access to an indoor pool and hot tub. Some have balcony and views.

Snow Valley Lodging — MOTEL $$

(☎877-696-7669; www.snowvalleymotel.com; 1041 7th Ave/Hwy 3; r from $99; 🅿🐕❄🀫) Great value in the middle of town. There are rooms, 'tiny homes' and suites that you can pick online and book direct. Throw in complimentary laundry facilities, bike use, BBQ area and hot tub and you have a great place to stay in Fernie.

🍴 Eating & Drinking

Blue Toque Diner — CAFE $

(☎250-423-4637; www.bluetoquediner.com; 601 1st Ave; mains from $12; ⏱9am-2:30pm Thu-Mon; 🀫) Part of the Arts Station community gallery, this is *the* place for breakfast. The menu features lots of seasonal and organic vegetarian specials.

★ Nevados Tapas & Tequila — LATIN AMERICAN $$

(☎250-423-5566; www.nevados.ca; 531 2 Ave; tapas from $4.50; ⏱5-10pm) The hottest spot in Fernie, Nevados is invitingly dark inside with century-old exposed-brick walls and a lovely outside terrace for long summer evenings. It's all on here, with a two-page tequila menu, local craft beers and a delightful selection of Latin tapas and full meals. Try the pork *arepa,* street food from Venezuela.

★ Yamagoya — JAPANESE $$

(☎250-430-0090; www.yamagoya.ca; 741 7th Ave/Hwy 3; small dishes from $4, mains from $11; ⏱5-10pm) As compact as a California roll, this gem of a sushi place serves a wide range of classics, from sashimi to tempura. The miso soup is good, especially after a day of skiing. In addition to sake, there's a great beer selection. Also has outdoor seating.

Fernie Distillers — DISTILLERY

(www.ferniedistillers.com; 531 1st Ave; ⏱4-10pm Wed-Fri, from 2pm Sat & Sun) Fernie's distillery sits next to the old station building and

Chairlift at Fernie Alpine Resort
SNOWLIZARD/GETTY IMAGES ©

produces small-batch (200 bottles per batch) hand-crafted gin and vodka. Turn up, view the stills, chat with the owners, sip the product and enjoy an extremely convivial laid-back atmosphere. The Prospector Gin and No 9 Mine Vodka are great, but don't forget to ask about the 'seasonal spirit'.

ℹ️ Information

Visitor Center (📞250-423-6868; www.fernie chamber.com; 102 Commerce Rd; ⏰9am-5pm Mon-Fri) Located east of town off Hwy 3, just past the Elk River crossing.

Kimberley

📞 250, 778 / POP 7425

When big-time mining left Kimberley in 1973, a plan was hatched to transform the little mountain village at 1113m altitude into the Bavarian City of the Rockies. The center became a pedestrian zone named the Platzl; locals were encouraged to prance about in lederhosen and dirndl; and sausage was added to many a menu. Now, more than three decades later, that shtick is long-gone, though the city still claims to have the largest freestanding cuckoo clock in Canada. There's still a bit of fake half-timbering here and there, but for the most part Kimberley is a diverse place that makes a worthwhile detour off Hwy 95 between Cranbrook and Radium Hot Springs.

Kimberley Alpine Resort   SKIING
(📞250-427-4881; www.skikimberley.com; 301 N Star Blvd; 1-day lift pass adult/child $75/30) In winter this popular resort has more than 700 hectares of skiable terrain, including 80 runs, and mild weather. Lots going on in summer including hiking, mountain biking, golf, canoeing, kayaking, rafting and fly-fishing.

Kimberley's Underground Mining Railway   RAIL
(📞250-427-7365; www.kimberleysunderground miningrailway.ca; Gerry Sorensen Way; adult/child $25/10; ⏰tours 11am, 1pm & 3pm May-Sep, trains to resort 10am Sat & Sun) Take a ride on Kimberley's Underground Mining Railway, where the tiny train putters through the steep-walled Mark Creek Valley toward some sweeping mountain vistas.

ℹ️ Information

Kimberley Visitor Centre (📞778-481-1891; www.tourismkimberley.com; 270 Kimberley Ave; ⏰10am-5pm daily Jul & Aug, closed Sun Sep-Jun) Has everything you need to know.

Cranbrook

📞 250, 778 / POP 19,250

The region's main center, 31km southeast of Kimberley, Cranbrook is a modest crossroads. Hwy 3/95 bisects the town and is lined with a charmless array of strip malls.

There are some surprisingly good drinking spots in Cranbrook, but you'll need to head into the older part of town, south of the highway.

⭐ **Cranbrook History Centre**   MUSEUM
(📞250-489-3918; www.cranbrookhistorycentre. com; 57 Van Horne St S, Hwy 3/95; adult/child $5/3; ⏰10am-5pm Tue-Sun) The one great reason for stopping in Cranbrook? This museum, which includes the Canadian Museum of Rail Travel. It has some fine examples of classic Canadian trains, including the luxurious 1929 edition of the Trans-Canada Limited, a legendary train that ran from Montréal to Vancouver.

Lazy Bear Lodge   MOTEL $
(📞250-426-6086; www.lazybear.ca; 621 Cranbrook Street N; r from $75; 🅿️❄️🔆🛜) Unlike most of the chain places along Hwy 95, locally owned Lazy Bear has been catering to visitors for nigh on 50 years. Nothing fancy, but its motel-type rooms are clean and affordable, plus there's a nice outdoor pool.

⭐ **Fire Hall Kitchen & Tap**   GASTROPUB $$
(📞778-520-0911; www.firehallcbk.ca; 37 11 Ave St; dinner mains from $12; ⏰8am-10pm Sun-Thu, to midnight Fri & Sat) Top BC craft beers (20 on tap!) and great food all day in what used to be Cranbrook's fire station. Rooftop and streetside seating, plus a beautifully renovated interior, make this an extremely atmospheric place to eat and drink.

Cranbrook to Rossland

Hwy 3 twists and turns its way 300km from Cranbrook to Osoyoos at the south end of the Okanagan Valley. Along the way it hugs the hills close to the US border and passes eight border crossings.

Creston, 123km west of Cranbrook, is known for its many orchards and as the home of Columbia Brewing Co's Kokanee True Ale. Hwy 3A heads north from here for a scenic 80km to the free Kootenay Lake Ferry, which connects to Nelson. This is a fun and scenic journey.

Some 85km west of Creston, Salmo is notable mostly as the junction with Hwy 6, which runs north for a bland 40km to Nelson. The Crowsnest Hwy splits 10km to the west. Hwy 3 bumps north through Castlegar, which has the closest large airport to Nelson and a very large pulp mill. Hwy 3B dips down through cute cafe-filled town Fruitvale and industrial Trail.

🛏 Sleeping & Eating

Each town on this route has at least a motel or two and basic road-trip treats are easily found. Creston has several fruit stands.

Valley View Motel MOTEL $
(☑ 250-428-2336; www.valleyviewmotel.info; 216 Valley View Dr, Creston; r from $75; P ⊝ ☒ 🛜) In motel-ville Creston, this is your best bet. On a view-splayed hillside, it's clean, comfortable and quiet.

Retro Cafe FRENCH $
(☑ 250-428-2726; www.retrocafe.ca; 1431 NW Blvd, Creston; mains from $8; ⊙ 7am-4pm Mon-Fri, to 3pm Sat) A French mirage in Creston, 'retro' will probably be the last thing on your mind as you scour the hand-scrawled blackboard and tuck into *très délicieux* crepes.

Rossland

☑ 250, 778 / POP 3730

Rossland is a world apart. High in the Southern Monashee Mountains (1023m), this old mining village is one of Canada's best places for mountain biking. A long history of mining has left the hills crisscrossed with old trails and abandoned rail lines, all of which are perfect for riding.

Free-riding is all the rage as the ridgelines are easily accessed and there are lots of rocky paths for plunging downhill. The Seven Summits & Dewdney Trail is a 35.8km singletrack along the crest of the Rossland Range. The Kootenay Columbia Trails Society (www.kcts.ca) has good maps online.

Red Mountain Ski Resort SKIING
(☑ 250-362-7384, snow report 250-362-5500; www.redresort.com; Hwy 3B; 1-day lift pass adult/child $96/48) Red Mountain Ski Resort draws mountain bikers in summer and plenty of ski enthusiasts in winter. Red, as it's called, includes the 1590m-high Red Mountain, the 2075m-high Granite Mountain and the 2048m-high Grey Mountain, for a total of 1670 hectares of challenging, powdery terrain

and 110 runs. Plenty going on with heli-, cat-, cross-country and backcountry skiing too.

**Flying Steamshovel
Gastropub & Inn** INN $
(☑ 250-362-7323; www.theflyingsteamshovel.com; 2003 2 Ave; r from $80; ⊝ 🛜) Lots going on here at the Flying Steamshovel, from the main street in Rossland. Great location, comfortable rooms, free parking – and if you're into craft beer, 14 different brews on tap. The restaurant offers a huge variety from its *poke* bowl to yellow coconut curry to the John Candy burger. Check the website for live concert listings.

ℹ Information

Rossland Visitor Centre (☑ 250-362-7722; www.rosslandmuseum.ca; 1100 Hwy 3B, Rossland Museum; ⊙ 11am-5pm May-Sep) Located in the Rossland Museum building, at the junction of Hwy 22 (coming from the US border) and Hwy 3B.

Nelson

☑ 250, 778 / POP 10,660

With plenty of cafes, culture and nightlife to keep you busy, Nelson makes a great base for visiting the nearby lakes. Best of all is the town's unique vibe, which is best experiences on Baker St, where wafts of patchouli mingle with hints of fresh-roasted coffee.

◉ Sights

More than 350 of Nelson's historic buildings have been carefully preserved and restored. Pick up the superb *Heritage Walking Tour* from the visitor center (p76) for a crash course in Victorian architecture.

By the iconic Nelson Bridge, Lakeside Park (Lakeside Dr; P) is a flower-filled, shady park and a beach. It has a great summer cafe.

**Touchstones Nelson
Museum of Art & History** MUSEUM
(☑ 250-352-9813; www.touchstonesnelson.ca; 502 Vernon St; adult/child $8/6; ⊙ 10am-5pm Mon-Wed, Fri & Sat, to 8pm Thu, to 4pm Sun Jun-Aug, closed Mon Sep-May) An enormous renovation transformed what was once a baronial old city hall (1902) into Touchstones Nelson, a museum of local history and art. Every month brings new exhibitions, many of which celebrate local artists. The history displays are engaging and interactive, banishing images of musty piles of poorly labeled artifacts.

🏃 Activities

From the center, follow the Waterfront Pathway, which runs along the length of the shore – its western extremity passes the airport and has a remote river vantage. You might choose to walk to Lakeside Park (p73) and then ride Streetcar 23 back along the 2km track from the park to the wharf at Hall St.

★ Kokanee Glacier
Provincial Park   HIKING
(www.env.gov.bc.ca/bcparks; Kokanee Glacier Rd) This park boasts 85km of some of the area's most superb hiking trails. The fantastic summer-only 2.5km (two-hour) round-trip hike to Kokanee Lake on a well-marked trail can be continued to the treeless, boulder-strewn expanse around the glacier. Turn off Hwy 3A 20.5km northeast of Nelson, then head another 16km on Kokanee Glacier Rd.

Whitewater
Winter Resort   SKIING
(☏ 250-354-4944, snow report 250-352-7669; www.skiwhitewater.com; off Hwy 6; 1-day lift ticket adult/child $76/38) Known for its heavy powdery snowfall, this laid-back resort 12km south of Nelson off Hwy 6 has small-town charm. Lifts are few, but so are the crowds, who enjoy a drop of 623m on 81 runs. There are 11 groomed Nordic trails.

Sacred Ride   MOUNTAIN BIKING
(☏ 250-354-3831; www.sacredride.ca; 213 Baker St; bicycle rental per day from $45; ☺ 9am-5:30pm Mon-Sat) The Sacred Ride has a wide variety of rentals. Also sells *Your Ticket to Ride,* an extensive trail map.

ROAM   KAYAKING
(Rivers, Oceans & Mountains; ☏ 250-354-2056; www.roamshop.com; 639 Baker St; kayak rental per day $40; ☺ 8am-7pm Mon-Sat, to 5pm Sun) ROAM sells and rents gear and offers advice. Book Kootenay Kayak Company (☏ 250-505-4549; www.kootenaykayak.com; kayak rentals per day $40-50, tours from $55) tours here.

Streetcar 23   RAIL
(☏ 250-352-7672; www.nelsonstreetcar.org; Waterfront Pathway; adult/child $3/2; ☺ 11am-4:30pm mid-May–mid-Nov) One of the town's originals, streetcar 23 follows a 2km track from Lakeside Park to the wharf at the foot of Hall St.

Great Northern Rail Trail   HIKING
Extending 42km from Nelson to Salmo along an old rail line, this trail has stunning views amid thick forest. Turn back whenever you want, but the first 6km have many highlights. The trailhead is at the corner of Cherry and Gore Sts.

🛏 Sleeping

Stay in the heart of Nelson so you can fully enjoy the city's beat.

★ Dancing Bear Inn   HOSTEL $
(☏ 250-352-7573; www.dancingbearinn.com; 171 Baker St; dm/r from $29/59; P☺🕱) 🖉 The brilliant management here offers advice and smooths the stay of guests in the 14 shared and private rooms, all of which share baths. There's a gourmet kitchen, library, patio and laundry.

★ Adventure Hotel   HOTEL $$
(☏ 250-352-7211; www.adventurehotel.ca; 616 Vernon St; r from $95; P☺✳🕱) Rooms come in three flavors at this well-located, slick, renovated hotel: budget (tiny, two bunk beds, shower down the hall), economy (full private bath) and deluxe (a choice of beds). Common areas include a lounge, patio, gym and rooftop sauna. The building also features the hotel's Uptown Sports Bar, Louie's Steakhouse and Empire Coffee café.

Hume Hotel & Spa   HOTEL $$
(☏ 250-352-5331; www.humehotel.com; 422 Vernon St; r incl breakfast from $120; P☺✳🕱) This 1898 classic hotel maintains its period grandeur. The 43 rooms vary greatly in shape and size; ask for the huge corner rooms with views of the hills and lake. Rates include a delicious breakfast. It has several appealing nightlife venues.

Victoria Falls
Guest House   INN $$
(☏ 250-551-3663; www.victoriafallsguesthouse.com; 213 Victoria St; r from $95; P☺🕱) The wide porch wraps right around this festive, yellow, renovated Victorian. The five suites have sitting areas and cooking facilities. Decor ranges from cozy antiques to family-friendly bunk beds. There is a barbecue.

Cloudside Hotel   B&B $$
(☏ 800-596-2337; www.cloudside.ca; 410 Victoria St; r from $125; P☺✳🕱) Live like a silver baron at this vintage mansion, where the eight rooms are named after trees. Luxuries abound, and a fine patio looks over the terraced gardens and the town. Check out and choose your room online.

✕ Eating & Drinking

Cottonwood Community Market MARKET $
(www.ecosociety.ca; 199 Carbonate St, Cottonwood Falls Park; ⊙ 9:30am-3pm Sat mid-May–Oct)
Close to downtown and next to the surging Cottonwood waterfall, this market encapsulates Nelson. There's great organic produce; fine baked goods, many with heretofore-unheard-of grains; and various craft items with artistic roots in tie-dyeing. A second event is the Downtown Market (Hall St; ⊙ 9:30am-3pm Wed mid-Jun–Sep).

Full Circle Cafe DINER $
(☑ 250-354-4458; www.facebook.com/fullcirclecafe; 402 Baker S; mains from $8; ⊙ 6:30am-2:30pm) A downtown diner beloved for its omelets, the Full Circle will have you doing just that as you return for skillfully made breakfast classics, such as eggs Benedict. It gets popular on weekends, so prepare for a wait.

★ Jackson's Hole & Grill CANADIAN $$
(☑ 250-354-1919; www.jacksonsgrill.ca; 524 Vernon St; dinner mains from $14; ⊙ 11:30am-9pm Sun-Tue, to 10pm Wed & Thu, to midnight Fri & Sat) In a historic building that has been around since 1897, this place is both lively and friendly. Used as Dixie's Café in the Steve Martin and Darryl Hannah Hollywood classic *Roxanne* in 1986, Jackson's serves soups, salads, sandwiches, wraps, burgers and pastas. Plenty to choose from in a very convivial atmosphere.

Cantina del Centro MEXICAN $$
(☑ 250-352-3737; www.cantinadelcentro.ca; 565 Baker St; small plates from $6; ⊙ 11am-late) Bright and vibrant, Cantina del Centro gets jammed with diners. The tacos and other small plates reflect the vivid colors of the Mexican tile floor. You can watch your meal being grilled behind the counter while you chill with a margarita. Opt for the buzz of an outdoor table.

★ Backroads Brewing Company MICROBREWERY
(☑ 778-463-3361; www.backroadsbrewing.com; 460 Baker St; ⊙ noon-10pm Mon-Thu, to 11pm Fri & Sat, to 8pm Sun) Nelson's local brews from tank to tap on Baker St. Small-batch, hand-crafted ales and lagers such as the El Dorado Golden Ale and Navigator Irish Red keep the locals coming back for more. Limited food apart from bar snacks, but that's not what you're here for, right?

Royal on Baker BAR
(☑ 250-354-7014; www.royalgrillnelson.com; 330 Baker St; ⊙ 5pm-2am) This gritty old pub on Baker gets some of the region's best music acts. It has a whole section of tables outside on the street and serves decent pub food.

Oso Negro Café CAFE
(☑ 250-532-7761; www.osonegrocoffee.com; 604 Ward St; ⊙ 7am-6pm; 🛜) This local favorite corner cafe roasts its own coffee in

Fall colors in Nelson

20 blends. Outside there are tables in a garden that burbles with water features amid statues. Enjoy baked goods and other snacks.

🛍 Shopping

Still Eagle Planetary
Persuasions   HOMEWARES
(☎ 250-352-3844; www.stilleagle.com; 421 Baker St; ⊙ 9am-7pm) ✦ Fair-trade and Kootenay-produced clothing, kitchen goods and products for the home are sold in this large store, which has a deep environmental commitment. Many products are made from recycled materials.

ℹ Information

Discover Nelson Visitor Centre (☎ 250-352-3433; www.discovernelson.com; 90 Baker St; ⊙ 8:30am-6pm daily May-Oct, to 5pm Mon-Fri Nov-Apr) Housed in the beautifully restored train station, it offers excellent brochures detailing driving and walking tours, plus has an excellent cafe.

ℹ Getting There & Away

West Kootenay Regional Airport (www.wkr airport.ca; Hwy 3A) The closest major airport to Nelson is 42km southwest at Castlegar.
West Kootenay Transit System (☎ 855-993-3100; www.bctransit.com; fares $2) The main stop is at the corner of Ward and Baker Sts.

Nelson to Revelstoke

Heading north from Nelson to Revelstoke, there are two options, both scenic. Hwy 6 heads west for 16km before turning north at South Slocan. The road eventually runs alongside pretty Slocan Lake for about 30km before reaching New Denver, 97km from Nelson.

The most interesting route is north and east from Nelson on Hwy 3A. Head 34km northeast to Balfour, where the free Kootenay Lake Ferry connects to Kootenay Bay. The ferry's worthwhile for its long lake vistas of blue mountains rising sharply from the water. From Kootenay Bay, Hwy 3A heads 80km south to Creston. Continuing north from the ferry at Balfour, the road becomes Hwy 31 and follows the lake 34km to Kaslo, passing cute towns. West from Kaslo to New Denver on Rte 31A is spectacular. North of there you pass Nakusp village and another free ferry before reaching Revelstoke. This is a great all-day trip.

ℹ Kootenay Ferries

The long Kootenay and Upper and Lower Arrow Lakes necessitate some scenic travel on inland ferries. On busy summer weekends, you may have to wait in a long line for a sailing or two before you get passage.

Kootenay Lake Ferry (☎ 250-229-215; www2.gov.bc.ca/gov/content/transportation/passenger-travel) sails between Balfour on the west arm of Kootenay Lake (34km northeast of Nelson) and Kootenay Bay, where you can follow Hwy 3A for the pretty 80km ride south to Creston. It is a 35-minute crossing. Departs Balfour every 50 minutes from 6:30am to 9:40pm, and Kootenay Lake from 7:10am to 10:20pm.

Needles Ferry (☎ 250-837-8418; ⊙ every 30mins, 24hr) crosses Lower Arrow Lake between Fauquier (57km south of Nakusp) and Needles (135km east of Vernon) on Hwy 6. The trip takes five minutes. This is a good link between the Okanagan Valley and the Kootenays.

Upper Arrow Lake Ferry (☎ 250-837-8418) runs between Galena Bay (49km north of Nakusp) and Shelter Bay (49km south of Revelstoke) on Hwy 23. The trip takes 20 minutes and runs from 5am to midnight every hour from Shelter Bay and every hour between 5:30am and 12:30am from Galena Bay.

Kootenay Lake Ferry
GIBSONPICTURES/GETTY IMAGES ©

Kaslo

A cute little town, Kaslo is an underrated gem with a beautiful lakeside setting.

Front Street has several good cafes and places for coffee.

SS Moyie
HISTORIC SITE

(☏ 250-353-2525; www.klhs.bc.ca; 324 Front St; adult/child $12/5; ☺10am-5pm mid-May–mid-Oct) Don't miss the restored 1898 lake steamer SS *Moyie*. It also has tourist info on the myriad ways to kayak and canoe the sparkling-blue waters.

Kaslo Hotel & Pub
HOTEL $$

(☏ 250-353-7714; www.kaslohotel.com; 430 Front St; r from $125; ⊖❋☎) This appealing three-story downtown veteran (1896) has lake views and a good pub. Rooms have balcony and porch.

New Denver

Wild mountain streams are just some of the spectacular highlights on Hwy 31A, which goes up and over some rugged hills west of Kaslo. At the end of this twisting 47km road, you reach New Denver, which seems about five years away from ghost-town status. But that's not necessarily bad, as this historic little gem slumbers away peacefully right on the clear waters of Slocan Lake. The equally sleepy old mining town of Silverton is just south.

Silvery Slocan Museum
MUSEUM

(☏ 250-358-2201; www.newdenver.ca/silvery-slocan-museum; 202 6th Ave; by donation; ☺9am-5pm daily Jul & Aug, Sat & Sun only Sep-Jun) Housed in the 1897 Bank of Montreal building, this museum features well-done displays from the booming mining days, a tiny vault and an untouched tin ceiling. It also has visitor info.

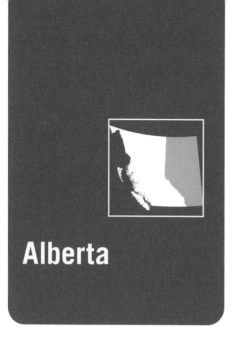

Alberta

Alberta does lakes and mountains like Rome does cathedrals and chapels, but without the penance. For proof head west to Jasper and Banff, two of the world's oldest national parks; despite their wild and rugged terrain, they remain untrammeled and easily accessible. They're majestic, breathtaking, awesome. No one should leave without first laying eyes on Peyto Lake and the Columbia Icefield.

ℹ️ Information

Travel Alberta (☎ 800-252-3782; www.travel alberta.com) Links to info on parks and visitor centers across the province.

ℹ️ Getting There & Away

Alberta was designed with the automobile (and an unlimited supply of gas) in mind. There are high-quality, well-maintained highways and a network of back roads to explore. Towns will for the most part have services, regardless of population.

Be aware that in more remote areas, especially in the north, those services could be a large distance apart, and often you will be hours between cell service areas. Fill up your gas tank wherever possible and be prepared for possible emergencies with things like warm clothes and water.

CALGARY

☎ 403 / POP 1,240,000

Calgary will surprise you with its beauty, cool eateries, nightlife beyond honky-tonk, and long, worthwhile to-do list. Calgarians aren't known for their modesty; it's their self-love and can-do attitude that got them through disastrous flooding in 2013 and, in 2016, saw them helping residents of wildfire-stricken

Fort McMurray with unquestioning generosity. We mustn't forget – Calgary also hosted the highly successful 1988 Winter Olympics, elected North America's first Muslim mayor, and throws one of Canada's biggest festivals, the Calgary Stampede.

The city is waking up and smelling the single-origin home-roasted coffee, too, with top-notch craft bars, boutique shops, restaurants and entertainment venues exhibiting more color and experimentation. Long stretches of riverside jogging and even a lone surfing spot make for outdoor activities that other cities can't hold a candle to. The longer you stay, the more there is to surprise you.

History

From humble and relatively recent beginnings, Calgary has been transformed into a cosmopolitan modern city that has hosted an Olympics and continues to wield huge economic clout. Before the growth explosion, the Blackfoot people had called the area home for centuries. Eventually they were joined by the Sarcee and Stoney tribes on the banks of the Bow and Elbow Rivers.

In 1875 the North West Mounted Police (NWMP) built a fort and called it Fort Calgary after Calgary Bay on Scotland's Isle of Mull. The railroad followed a few years later and, buoyed by the promise of free land, settlers started the trek west to make Calgary their home. The Blackfoot, Sarcee and Stoney indigenous groups signed Treaty 7 with the British Crown in 1877, which ushered them into designated reservations and took away their wider land rights.

Long a center for ranching, the cowboy culture was set to become forever intertwined with the city. In the early 20th century, Calgary simmered along, growing slowly. Then, in the 1960s, everything changed. Overnight, ranching was seen as a thing of the past, and oil was the new favorite child. With the 'black gold' seeming to bubble up from the ground nearly everywhere in Alberta, Calgary became the natural choice of place to set up headquarters.

The population exploded, and the city began to grow at an alarming rate. As the price of oil continued to skyrocket, it was good times for the people of Cowtown. The 1970s boom stopped dead at the '80s bust. Things slowed and the city diversified.

The 21st century began with an even bigger boom. House prices have gone through the roof, there is almost zero unemployment and the economy is growing 40% faster than the rest of Canada. Not bad for a bunch of cowboys.

◉ Sights

Calgary's downtown has the Glenbow Museum and the National Music Centre, but it's the surrounding neighborhoods that hold more allure. **Uptown 17th Avenue** has some of the top restaurants and bars and is a hive of activity in the evening. **Inglewood**, just east of downtown, is the city's hippest neighborhood, with antique shops, indie boutiques and some esoteric eating options. **Kensington**, north of the Bow River, has some good coffee bars and a tangible community spirit.

★ National Music Centre   MUSEUM
(☑ 403-543-5115; http://nmc.ca; 850 4th St SE; adult/child $18/11; ⊘ 10am-5pm May-Aug, Wed-Sun Sep-Apr) Looking like a whimsical copper castle, this fabulous museum is entirely entertaining, taking you on a ride through Canada's musical history with rotating exhibits, cool artifacts (like the guitar Guess Who used to record 'American Woman') and interactive displays. Test your skill at the drums, electric guitar or in a sound-recording room and

even create your own instruments. Don't miss the Body Phonic room or the solar-powered Skywalk with its repurposed pianos destroyed in the 2013 flood.

You don't need to be a music junkie to enjoy yourself here, but you'll probably leave as one. There's an excellent cafe on-site.

★ Glenbow Museum   MUSEUM
(☑ 403-777-5506; www.glenbow.org; 130 9th Ave SE; adult/child/family $18/11/45; ⊘ 9am-5pm Mon-Sat, noon-5pm Sun, closed Mon Oct-Jun) With an extensive permanent collection and an ever-changing array of traveling exhibitions, the impressive Glenbow has plenty for the history buff, art lover and pop-culture fiend to ponder. Temporary exhibits are often daring, covering contemporary art and culture. Permanent exhibits bring the past to life with strong historic personalities and lots of voice recordings. Hang out in a tipi, visit a trading post and walk through the railcar of a train.

Esker Foundation Contemporary Art Gallery   MUSEUM
(https://eskerfoundation.com; 1011 9th Ave SE, Inglewood; ⊘ 11am-6pm Sun, Tue & Wed, to 8pm Thu & Fri) FREE This small, private art gallery hosts fabulous temporary exhibitions in its beautiful 4th-floor location. Past exhibitions have considered everything from immigration to the Northwest Passage. Check the website for workshops and be sure to check out the very cool boardroom nest.

Prince's Island Park

ALBERTA CALGARY

Map labels

1 KENSINGTON

NB Sunnyside

11th St NW
10A St NW
10th St NW
C-Train

Memorial Dr
Peace Bridge
Bow River

5

2
7

Louise Bridge

Eau Claire Ave SW
1st Ave SW
2nd Ave SW
3rd Ave SW

9
19
6

10

3rd St SW

4th Ave SW

5th Ave SW

DOWNTOWN

3
WB Downtown - West Kerby
4
6th Ave SW
7th Ave SW   WB 7 St SW   WB 4 St SW   C-Train   WB 1 St SW
8th St SW   EB 6 St SW   EB 3 St SW
8th Ave SW   Stephen Ave Walk
24   11

9th Ave SW

26

4
10th Ave SW
22
DESIGN DISTRICT
11th Ave SW
12th Ave SW
6th St SW
BELTLINE

12th St SW
11th St SW
10th St SW
9th St SW
8th St SW
13th Ave SW
14th Ave SW
13
5th St SW
4th St SW
2nd St SW
1st St SW
21

5
12
15th Ave SW
20
18   14
17   15
16th Ave SW
17th Ave SW
18th St SW
7th St SW
UPTOWN 17TH AVE
18th Ave SW
19th Ave SW

Prince's Island Park   PARK

For a little slice of Central Park in the heart of Cowtown, take the bridge over to this island, with grassy fields made for tossing Frisbees, plus bike paths and ample space to stretch out. During the summer months, you can catch a Shakespeare production in the park's natural grass amphitheater or check out the Folk Music Festival (p83) in July. You'll also find the upscale River Island restaurant here.

Watch yourself around the river. The water is cold and the current is strong and not suitable for swimming. The bridge to the island from downtown is at the north end of 3rd St SW, near the Eau Claire Market shopping area.

Heritage Park
Historical Village   HISTORIC SITE

(403-268-8500; www.heritagepark.ca; 1900 Heritage Dr SW, at 14th St SW; adult/child $26.25/13.65; 10am-5pm daily May-Aug, Sat & Sun Sep & Oct;) Want to see what Calgary used to look like? Head down to this historical park (the largest in Canada!) where all the buildings are from 1915 or earlier. There are 10 hectares of recreated town to explore, with a

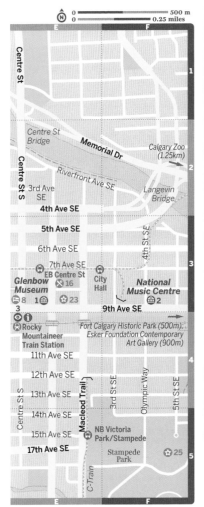

0		500 m
0		0.25 miles

Calgary

Top Sights
1 Glenbow Museum..............................E3
2 National Music Centre.......................F3

◎ **Sights**
3 Calgary Tower..................................E4
4 Contemporary Calgary.....................A3
5 Prince's Island Park..........................D1

Activities, Courses & Tours
6 Eau Claire Rapid Rent.......................D2

Sleeping
7 Hotel Arts Kensington.......................A2
8 Hotel Le Germain.............................E3

◎ **Eating**
9 1886 Buffalo Cafe.............................D2
10 Alforno Cafe & Bakery......................C2
11 Blink..D3
12 Galaxie Diner...................................A5
13 Jelly Modern Doughnuts...................B4
14 Market...C5
15 Ox Bar de Tapas..............................C5
16 Teatro..E3
17 Una..C5

Drinking & Nightlife
18 Analog Coffee...................................C5
19 Barley Mill.......................................D2
20 Betty Lou's Library...........................B5
21 Pr%f...D4
22 Twisted Element...............................B4

◎ **Entertainment**
23 Arts Commons..................................E3
24 Globe Cinema...................................C3
25 Saddledome......................................F5

◎ **Shopping**
26 Mountain Equipment Co-op..............B4

ALBERTA CALGARY

Calgary Zoo   ZOO
(☑403-232-9300; www.calgaryzoo.com; 1300 Zoo
Rd NE; adult/child $37/27; ⊙9am-5pm; ▣) More
than 1000 animals from around the world,
many in enclosures simulating their natural
habitats, make Calgary's zoo one of the top rated in North America. The zoo's well-regarded
conservation team study, reintroduce and
protect endangered animals in Canada.

Besides the animals, the zoo has a Botanical Garden, with changing garden displays,
a tropical rainforest, a good butterfly
enclosure and the 6½-hectare Prehistoric
Park, featuring fossil displays and life-
size dinosaur replicas in natural settings.
There's also a captive breeding program

fort, grain mill, church and school. Go for a
hay ride, visit the antique midway or hop on
a train. Costumed interpreters are on hand
to answer any questions.

You can ride on the steam train, catch a trol-
ley and even go for a spin on the SS *Moyie,* the
resident stern-wheeler, as it churns around
the Glenmore Reservoir. Heritage Park has
always been a big hit with the kiddies and is
a great place to soak up Western culture. To
get there, take the C-Train to Heritage station,
then bus 502. The park is 10km south of Calgary's downtown. It is a registered charity, so
your money is going to a good cause.

for whooping cranes. Picnic areas, concessions and cafes dot the zoo. During winter, when neither you nor the animals will care to linger outdoors, the admission price is reduced. To get here, take the C-Train east to the Zoo stop.

Calgary Tower
NOTABLE BUILDING

(☑403-266-7171; www.calgarytower.com; 101 9th Ave SW; adult/youth $18/9; ⊙observation gallery 9am-9pm Sep-Jun, to 10pm Jul & Aug) This 1968 landmark tower is an iconic feature of the Calgary skyline, though it has now been usurped by numerous taller buildings and is in danger of being lost in a forest of skyscrapers. There is little doubt that the aesthetics of this once-proud concrete structure have passed into the realm of kitsch, but, love it or hate it, the slightly phallic 191m structure is a fixture of the downtown area.

Telus Spark
MUSEUM

(☑403-817-6800; www.sparkscience.ca; 220 St George's Dr NE; adult/child $26/19, plus $10 parking; ⊙10am-5pm; 🚼) You'll wish science class was as fun as the Telus Spark. Kids get a big bang out of this user-friendly and very interactive science center. There is a giant dome, where light shows depicting the cosmos are projected, and a whole raft of other things to discover. Adults Only Nights (random Thursdays) let the 18-plus crowd experience the place without kids.

Contemporary Calgary
GALLERY

(☑403-770-1350; www.contemporarycalgary.com; 701 11th St SW; ⊙noon-6pm Wed-Sun)  This inspiring modern-art gallery has three floors of temporary exhibits that change every four months. The gallery is now in the former Centennial Planetarium in the southwest of Calgary, with displays of modern and contemporary art. The building itself is famous for its brutalist-style architecture.

🏃 Activities & Tours

Eau Claire Rapid Rent
CYCLING

(☑403-444-5845; Barclay Pde SW; bikes/rollerblades/helmet per day from $40/25/7; ⊙10am-6pm May-Sep) Rents out bikes, junior bikes, tandem bikes, child trailers and rollerblades. And rafts, if you happen to have a car and trailer.

Olympic Oval
ICE SKATING

(☑403-220-7954; www.ucalgary.ca/oval; 288 Collegiate Blvd NW, University of Calgary; adult/child/family $7/5/18.50; ⊙Aug–mid-Mar) Get the Olympic spirit at the University of Calgary, where you can go for a skate on Olympic Oval. Used for the speed-skating events at the Olympics, it offers public skating on the long track and has skates available to rent, as well as mandatory helmets. See the website for current schedules.

CYCLING THE ICEFIELDS PARKWAY

With its ancient geology, landscape-altering glaciers, and lakes bluer than Picasso paintings from his blue period, the 230km-long Icefields Parkway is one of the world's most spectacular roads, and, by definition, one of the world's most spectacular bicycle rides – if your legs and lungs are up to it. Aside from the distance, there are several long uphill drags, occasional stiff headwinds and two major passes to contend with, namely Bow Summit (2088m) and Sunwapta Pass (2035m). Notwithstanding these issues, the route is highly popular in July and August (don't even think about doing it in the winter), with aspiring cyclists lapping up its bicycle-friendly features. No commercial trucks are allowed on the parkway, there's a generous shoulder throughout, two-wheeled company is virtually guaranteed, and accommodations along the route (campgrounds, hostels and the occasional lodge or hotel) are plentiful and strategically placed. There's a choice of six HI hostels and four lodge/motel accommodations en route. Book ahead. Basic provisions can be procured at Saskatchewan River Crossing, 83km north of Lake Louise.

Sturdy road bikes can be rented from Wilson Mountain Sports (☑403-522-3636; www.wmsll.com; Samson Mall, Lake Louise village; bike/ski rental per day from $39/25; ⊙8am-7pm) in Lake Louise village. Brewster (☑403-221-8242; www.banffjaspercollection.com/brewster-express; 100 Gopher St; adult/child Banff to Calgary Airport $72/36, to Jasper $120/60, to Lake Louise $37/19) buses can sometimes transport bicycles, but always check ahead. Backroads (☑510-527-1555; www.backroads.com; 5-day tour from $3449) runs a Canadian Rockies Bike Tour, a six-day organized trip that incorporates cycling along the parkway.

CAR-LESS IN CALGARY

As the main operations center for Canada's oil industry, Calgary has a reputation for big, unsubtle automobiles plying endless low-rise suburbs on a network of busy highways. But, hidden from the ubiquitous petrol heads is a parallel universe of urban parkways (712km of 'em!) dedicated to walkers, cyclists and skaters, and many of them hug the banks of the city's two mighty rivers, the Bow and the Elbow. Even better, this non-car-traffic network is propped up by a cheap, efficient light-rail system: the C-Train carries a number of daily riders comparable to the Amsterdam metro. Yes, dear reader, Calgary without a car is not an impossible – or even unpleasant – experience.

Not surprisingly, the best trails hug the riverbanks. The Bow River through downtown and over into Prince's Island is eternally popular, with the pedestrian-only Peace Bridge providing a vital link. If you're feeling strong, you can follow the river path 20km south to Fish Creek Provincial Park and plenty more roadless action. Nose Creek Parkway is the main pedestrian artery to and from the north of the city, while the leafy Elbow River Pathway runs from Inglewood to Mission in the south.

Abutting the downtown Bow River Pathway is Eau Claire Rapid Rent, located next to the Eau Claire shopping center.

The city publishes an official *Calgary Pathways and Bikeways* map available from any local leisure center or downloadable from the City of Calgary website (www.calgary.ca). There's also a mobile app at www.calgary.ca/mobileapps.

Calgary Walking Tours CULTURAL
(☑ 855-620-6520; www.calgarywalks.com; adult/under 3yr/youth $28/free/18) Join the two-hour Downtown City tour to learn about the architecture, history and culture of various buildings, sculptures, gardens and hidden nooks.

✨ Festivals & Events

For a year-round list of the city's events, go to www.visitcalgary.com/things-to-do. The big festival in Calgary is the annual Calgary Stampede; however, there are many other smaller festivals, markets and exhibitions throughout the year.

Calgary Stampede RODEO
(☑ ticket office 403-269-9822; www.calgarystampede.com; adult/child $18/9; ⊘ 2nd week Jul) Billed as the greatest outdoor show on earth, rodeos don't come much bigger than the Calgary Stampede. Daily shows feature bucking broncos, steer wrestling, chuckwagon races, a midway and a sensational grandstand show. Civic spirits soar, with free pancake breakfasts and a cowboy hat on every head in the city. All of this is strongly tempered by animal rights issues.

Each year, numerous animals are injured and several are put down. Humane societies and animal rights activists strongly oppose endangering animals for entertainment and money-making, and spotlight calf roping and chuckwagon races as two of the most dangerous activities at the Stampede. In 2019 three horses died.

Countering that grim reality is the fact that these same chuckwagon races often allow thoroughbred horses that would have been euthanized immediately after suffering injuries on the horse track to live on for years, even decades, doing what they love most: racing. The owners don't always like the term 'rescue' horse, but it's often true. So the Stampede is a complex, multifaceted issue and a personal one. If you do decide to go to the rodeo, be prepared for the possibility of an injury to happen before your very eyes. There are lots of other entertainment options: rides, amusements and games. But the tradition has always been the rodeo.

If you do decide to visit Calgary during Stampede, book ahead for accommodations and prepare to pay premium prices: nearly every hotel will be full, and rates go through the roof.

Calgary Folk Music Festival MUSIC
(www.calgaryfolkfest.com; ⊘ late Jul) Grassroots folk is celebrated at this annual four-day event featuring great live music on Prince's Island. Top-quality acts from around the globe make the trek to Cowtown. It's a mellow scene hanging out on the grass listening to the sounds of summer with what seems like 12,000 close friends. Tickets per day are around $85 or it's $195 for all four days.

🛏 Sleeping

Calgary has a range of hotels across different price ranges, as well as a few hostels close to or in downtown.

Downtown is pricey, although many hotels run frequent specials. Business-oriented hotels are often cheaper over weekends. Near the city's western edge (near the Banff Trail C-Train station), you'll find every chain hotel you can think of.

During the Calgary Stampede (early July), rates rise and availability plummets. Book ahead.

Calgary West Campground   CAMPGROUND $
(☑ 403-288-0411; www.calgarycampground.com; Hwy 1; tent/RV sites for 2 people $42/61, extra person $5; ⊙ mid-Apr–mid-Oct; P @ 🛜 ❋) Featuring terraced grounds with views across the city, this campground has sites with great facilities, including a heated outdoor pool, nature trails, mini-golf and free wi-fi. Situated west of downtown Calgary on the Trans-Canada Hwy (Hwy 1), it's a quick trip into the city.

⭐ Hotel Arts Kensington   BOUTIQUE HOTEL $$
(☑ 403-228-4442; www.hotelartskensington.com; 1126 Memorial Dr NW; r from $223; P ⊖ 🛜) This small inn remains a great spot across the river. Impeccable service and rooms to match, plus soaker tubs, fireplaces, balconies, French doors and fine linens are all to be found. It's a short trip over the bridge to downtown and the hotel restaurant is top-notch.

Hotel Alma   BOUTIQUE HOTEL $$
(☑ 403-220-3203; www.hotelalma.ca; 169 University Gate NW; r from $120, ste $180; ⊖ 🛜) Cleverly tucked away on the university campus, this fashionable boutique establishment has a definite hip vibe. Super-modern Euro-style rooms are small but cozy rather than cramped. The city suites have one bedroom and are lovely. Guests have a free breakfast, as well as access to on-campus facilities, including a fitness center and pool.

The university is 6km northwest of downtown, but is easily accessible on the C-Train (University stop).

Centro Motel   MOTEL $$
(☑ 403-288-6658; www.centromotel.com; 4540 16th Ave NW; r incl breakfast from $114; P ❋ @ 🛜) A 'boutique motel' sounds like an oxymoron until you descend on the misleadingly named Centro (not in the center at all!), an old motel building that has been transformed with modern features. Rooms are comfy, almost chic, and come with bathrobes and walk-in spa showers. You'll find it 7km northwest of downtown on the Trans-Canada Hwy (Hwy 1, aka 16th Ave).

In non-peak times (winter months, mainly) prices can drop by 20% to 30%. Staff are friendly and helpful.

⭐ Hotel Le Germain   BOUTIQUE HOTEL $$$
(☑ 403-264-8990; www.germaincalgary.com; 899 Centre St SW; d from $299; P ⊖ ❋ @ 🛜) 🏵 A posh boutique hotel to counteract the bland assortment of franchise inns that service downtown Calgary. Part of a small French-Canadian chain, the style verges on opulent. Rooms are elegant, while the 24-hour gym, in-room massage, complimentary newspapers and stylish lounge add luxury touches.

Even better, the hotel is efficiently built and has a long list of conservation policies.

🍴 Eating

Traditionalists still call it Cowtown, but dip your metaphoric fork into Calgary's fast-moving restaurant scene and you'll find that Albertan beef isn't the only thing propping up the menu these days. Calgary is Canada's third most cosmopolitan city after Toronto and Vancouver and the diversity is reflected in the food.

⭐ Alforno Cafe & Bakery   CAFE $
(☑ 403-454-0308; www.alforno.ca; 222 7th St SW; mains $9-21; ⊙ 7am-9pm Mon-Fri, 8am-9pm Sat, 8am-5pm Sun) This ultra-modern, super-comfortable cafe is the kind of place you'll want to hang out all day. Bellinis, beer on tap, carafes of wine and excellent coffee won't discourage you from lingering, nor will magazines, comfy sofas or window seats. With pastas, flatbreads, salads, soups and panini, all homemade, it's difficult to leave room for the amazing cakes, tarts and biscuits.

The sweets category includes espresso shortbread with caramelized sugar and chocolate cream puffs. Breakfasts tempt with eggs Bennie, smashed avocado toast and a bacon breakfast sandwich.

⭐ 1886 Buffalo Cafe   BREAKFAST $
(☑ 403-269-9255; www.1886buffalocafe.com; 187 Barclay Pde SW; breakfast mains $9-19; ⊙ 6am-3pm Mon-Fri, from 7am Sat & Sun) This is a true salt-of-the-earth diner in the high-rise-dominated city center. Built in 1911 and the only surviving building from the lumber

yard once here, the exterior's peeling clapboards sure make it look authentic. This is a ketchup on the table, unlimited coffee refills kind of place famous for its brunches, especially its huevos rancheros.

Galaxie Diner
DINER **$**

(☑403-228-0001; www.galaxiediner.ca; 1413 11th St SW; mains $12-18; ⊙7am-3pm Mon-Fri, to 4pm Sat & Sun) Looking more authentic than themed, this classic, no-nonsense 1950s diner serves all-day breakfasts, burgers and milkshakes. Squeeze into a booth, grab a seat at the bar or (more likely) join the queue at the door. The Calgary Sandwich, a scrumptious mix of just about everything under the sun, is a popular favorite, as are the extra-thick, ample-sized, made-to-order milkshakes.

Gravity Espresso & Wine Bar
CAFE **$**

(☑403-457-0697; www.cafegravity.com; 909 10th St SE; light lunches $7-12; ⊙8am-5pm Sun & Mon, to 10pm Tue-Thu, to midnight Fri & Sat) ✔ This hybrid cafe-bar, which alters its personality depending on the clientele and the time of day, is a thoughtful, community-led business. The crux of the operation is the locally roasted Phil & Sebastian coffee beans, but that's just an overture for loads of other stuff, including live acoustic music, curry nights, home-baked snacks and fund-raisers.

Jelly Modern Doughnuts
BAKERY **$**

(☑403-453-2053; www.jellymoderndoughnuts. com; 1414 8th St SW; doughnuts $2.50-3; ⊙7am-6pm Mon-Fri, 9am-6pm Sat, to 5pm Sun) Bright pink and sugary-smelling, Jelly Modern has grabbed the initiative on weird doughnut flavors. The maple and bacon or bourbon vanilla varieties won't help ward off any impending heart attacks, but they'll make every other doughnut you've ever tasted seem positively bland by comparison.

Everything's baked on-site, meaning once you've taken one sniff inside the glass door, you're putty in their hands. In addition to coffee, there are tasty options for tea drinkers, such as the 'London Fog,' a latte made with Earl Grey and frothed milk.

Ox Bar de Tapas
TAPAS **$$**

(☑403-457-1432; www.oxtapas.com; 528 17th Ave SW; tapas $5-18; ⊙5-11pm Sun, 4-10pm Tue-Thu, to midnight Fri & Sat) Recreating Spain in modern Calgary isn't an obvious go-to, but Ox Bar de Tapas has somehow managed it with colorful tiles and delicious tapas. Order piecemeal from a menu of Manchego

Galaxie Diner
JEFF WHYTE/SHUTTERSTOCK ©

cheese, tortilla (Spanish omelet) and cured *jamón serrano*.

Una
PIZZA **$$**

(☑403-453-1183; www.unapizzeria.com; 618 17th Ave SW; pizzas $17-24; ⊙11:30am-1am) There's often a line out the door but nobody seems to mind waiting – that's how good these thin-crust pizzas are. There's plenty of good house wine, too.

★Market
CANADIAN **$$$**

(☑403-474-4414; www.marketcalgary.ca; 718 17th Ave SW; mains lunch $19-26, dinner $18-42; ⊙11:30am-11pm) With an earthy yet futuristic feel, award-winning Market has gone a step further in the fresh-local trend. Not only does it bake its own bread, but it also butchers and cures meat, makes cheese and grows 16 varieties of heirloom seeds year-round. As if that weren't enough, it's then all whipped into meals that are scrumptious and entirely satisfying.

Look for dishes like truffle buttermilk chicken wings, hand-rolled pasta or duck waffles. There's also a $25 prix-fixe option...yum!

★Teatro
ITALIAN **$$$**

(☑403-290-1012; www.teatro.ca; 200 8th Ave SE; mains lunch $19-40, dinner $30-60; ⊙11:30am-3pm Mon-Fri, 5-10pm Sun-Thu, to 11pm Fri & Sat) In a regal bank building next to the Epcor Centre for the Performing Arts, Teatro has an art nouveau touch with its marble bar top, swirling metalwork and high-backed curved sofas. Dishes are works of art and fuse Italian influences, French nouvelle cuisine and a bit of traditional Alberta. Service is friendly and impeccable.

The wine list is fabulous and the chef's six-course tasting menu is an epic journey through the best parts of the fancy menu.

Blink
FUSION $$$

(☑ 403-263-5330; www.blinkcalgary.com; 111 8th Ave SW; mains $24-42; ⊙11am-2pm Mon-Fri, 5-10pm Mon-Sat) 🍴 It's true: you could miss this small oasis tucked along a busy street and that would be a shame. Inside this trendy gastro haven, an acclaimed chef oversees an ever-evolving menu of fine dishes like smoked ricotta ravioli with walnuts and truffle vinaigrette or grilled striploin with caramelized shallots and red-wine sauce. Food is fresh and, wherever possible, locally sourced.

Drinking & Nightlife

Craft cocktail, thy name is Calgary. Hit 17th Ave NW for a slew of martini lounges and crowded pubs, and 4th St SW for a lively after-work scene. There's even a password-protected speakeasy now. Other spots include Kensington Rd NW and Stephen Ave. Calgary's LGBTIQ+ scene is ever-improving; even the Stampede has a drag show now.

★ Betty Lou's Library
COCKTAIL BAR

(☑ 403-454-4774; www.bettylouslibrary.com; 908 17th Ave SW; ⊙5pm-12:30am Tue-Thu, to 2am Fri & Sat) Betty Lou's Library won't be for everyone, but if you like feeling like you've stepped back in time to Prohibition 1920s, then you'll get a kick out of coming here. The cocktails are superb; if you can't decide just ask one of the bartenders for a custom-crafted cup of yum. You'll need a password to enter, so call first.

The entrance is actually on 16th Ave, not 17th. Look for a red light, a bookshelf and a phone.

Note also that there are some house rules that are enforced – among them, no talking or making chitchat with other parties at the bar. That means this spot is best enjoyed with a friend or two, unless you like drinking alone.

★ Pr%f
COCKTAIL BAR

(☑ 403-246-2414; www.proofyyc.com; 1302 1st St SW; ⊙4pm-midnight Sun & Mon, to 1am Tue-Sat) No, that isn't a typo. Pr%f might be small but the bar is big enough to require a library lad-

der, and the drinks menu not only requires time, but also imagination. The menu itself is a beautiful thing to behold and the drinks look so stunning, you almost don't want to drink them. But you do. Trust us, you do.

Analog Coffee
COFFEE

(☑ 403-910-5959; www.analogcoffee.ca; 740 17th Ave SW; coffees $3-6; ⊙7am-10pm, to midnight Jul & Aug) The third-wave coffee scene is stirring in Calgary, led by companies like Fratello, which runs this narrow, overflowing hipster-ish 17th Ave cafe. Beans of the day are displayed on a clipboard and there are rows of retro vinyl along the back wall. Teas are here, too, as are tasty desserts aplenty.

Barley Mill
PUB

(☑ 403-290-1500; www.barleymillcalgary.com; 201 Barclay Pde SW; ⊙11am-midnight, from 10am Sun) Built in a 1900s style, with the original distillery's lumber used for the top floor and an actual waterwheel churning outside, the Barley Mill draws crowds for its pub grub, long lineup of draft beers and a well-stocked bar. Two patios for when it's warm and a big stone fireplace for when it's not keep it busy in every season.

Twisted Element
GAY & LESBIAN

(☑ 403-802-0230; www.twistedelement.ca; 1006 11th Ave SW; ⊙9pm-2am Wed-Sun) Consistently voted the best queer dance venue by the local community, this club has weekly drag shows, karaoke nights and DJs spinning nightly.

☆ Entertainment

Calgary has a lively and varied entertainment scene, from comedy shows and improv theater to Shakespeare and indie films only a Canadian could love.

Ironwood Stage & Grill
LIVE MUSIC

(☑ 403-269-5581; www.ironwoodstage.ca; 1229 9th Ave SE, Inglewood; ⊙shows 8pm Sun-Thu, 9pm Fri & Sat) Cross over into the hip universe of Inglewood to find the grassroots of Calgary's music scene, here inside the Garry Theatre. Local bands alternate with bigger touring acts for nightly music in the welcoming, woody confines of Ironwood. Country and folk are the staples. Events are all ages.

The dinner menu will make you want to eat a second dinner; it includes dishes like seafood risotto, Mediterranean lamb loaf and roasted portobello ratatouille.

Calgary Flames
SPECTATOR SPORT

(☎ 403-777-2177; http://flames.nhl.com) Archrival of the Edmonton Oilers, the Calgary Flames play ice hockey from October to April at the Saddledome (☎ 403-777-4646; Stampede Park). Make sure you wear red to the game and head down to 17th Ave afterward, or the 'Red Mile,' as they call it during play-offs.

Arts Commons
THEATER

(☎ 403-294-7455; https://artscommons.ca; 205 8th Ave SE) This is the hub for live theater in Calgary. With four theaters and one of the best concert halls in North America, you can see everything from ballet to Bollywood here.

Globe Cinema
CINEMA

(☎ 403-262-3309; www.globecinema.ca; 617 8th Ave SW; tickets $10; ⊘ 6:30-9:30pm, matinees Sat & Sun) This art-house theater specializes in foreign films and Canadian cinema – both often hard to find in mainstream movie houses. Look for discounts on Tuesdays and matinees on the weekend.

🛍 Shopping

Calgary has several hot shopping spots, but these districts are reasonably far apart. The Kensington area and 17th Ave SW have a good selection of interesting, fashionable clothing shops and funky trinket outlets. Stephen Ave Walk is a pedestrian mall with shops, bookstores and atmosphere. Inglewood is good for antiques, junk, apothecaries, and secondhand books and vinyl.

Tea Trader
TEA

(☎ 403-264-0728; www.teatrader.com; 1228a 9th Ave SE, Inglewood; ⊘ 10am-5pm Tue-Sat, noon-4pm Sun) This wonderful shop is up a set of stairs and very easy to miss, but it's worth searching out for its lovely aroma wafting around the room, cheery, happy-to-help proprietors and wealth of tea options. Teas from all over the world line the shelves, as well as some local flavors.

Alberta Boot Co
SHOES

(☎ 403-263-4623; www.albertaboot.com; 50 50th Ave SE; ⊘ 9am-6pm Mon-Sat) Visit the factory and store run by the province's only Western boot manufacturer and pick up a pair of your choice made of kangaroo, bullhide or boring old cowhide, or just breathe in the aroma of leather and tanning oil. Over 200 hours of labor go into each boot, and prices range from $385 to $2100 or more.

If the boots are too pricey, there are coasters at the door made from leather scraps that make a nice souvenir.

Smithbilt Hats
HATS

(☎ 403-244-9131; https://smithbilthats.com; 1015 11th St SE; ⊘ 9am-5pm Mon-Wed & Fri, to 7pm Thu, 10am-4pm Sat) Ever wondered how a cowboy hat is made? Here is your chance to find out. Smithbilt has been shaping hats in the traditional way since 1919 when you parked your horse out front. You can pick up one made of straw or beaver felt and priced accordingly, or just marvel at the artisans as they work, crafting, cutting and shaping.

Mountain Equipment Co-op
SPORTS & OUTDOORS

(☎ 403-269-2420; www.mec.ca; 830 10th Ave SW; ⊘ 10am-9pm Mon-Fri, 9am-6pm Sat, 10am-5pm Sun) MEC is the place to get your outdoor kit sorted before heading into the hills. It's a Canadian institution with a huge selection of outdoor equipment, travel gear, active clothing and books.

ⓘ Information

Rockyview General Hospital (☎ 403-943-3000; 7007 14th St SW; ⊘ 24hr) Emergency room open 24 hours.

Visit Calgary (www.visitcalgary.com; 101 9th Ave SW; ⊘ 8am-5pm) Operates a visitor center in the base of the Calgary Tower (p82). The staff can help you find accommodations. Information booths are also available at both the arrivals and departures levels of the airport.

Ironwood Stage & Grill
JEFF WHYTE/SHUTTERSTOCK ©

STRETCH YOUR LEGS CALGARY

Start/Finish: Fort Calgary

- -

Distance: 3.2km

- -

Duration: 4 hours

Calgary has tons of walking options, but this trip takes you through the Inglewood area, where shopping, great eats and pretty scenery all combine. Its duration really depends on how much time you spend at each stop.

FORT CALGARY

Park your car here and fill the meter with enough for you to spend a few hours inside **Fort Calgary Historic Park** (☑ 403-290-1875; www.fortcalgary.com; 750 9th Ave SE; adult/child $12/7; ☺ 9am-5pm). The site, occupied by a replica of a military barracks that stood here in the 1880s, is undergoing expansion, but there's a lot to see inside – exhibits of ranching and Western life, indigenous cultures and plenty more. There are ever-rotating exhibits and events as well, so give yourself plenty of time to check out what's here.

The Walk ≫ Refill your parking meter before heading out east, then turn left onto the Riverwalk.

RIVERWALK

This is just a **path**, but it's a pretty one, and it runs along the river. You can walk as long or as little as you like, with cyclists, walkers, families, dogs and kids. This one's essentially up to you.

The Walk ≫ When you're ready to keep going, return to the Inglewood Bridge and cross over on 9th Ave SE. Go a couple of blocks and you'll see Bite on your right.

BITE

Part-grocery, part-deli, part-restaurant, **Bite** (☑ 403-263-3966; http://biteyyc.com; 1023 9th Ave SE; mains $8-16; ☺ 8am-8pm Mon-Fri, to 6:30pm Sat & Sun) is a one-stop-fits-all place to have a nice brunch, a late snack or a cool refreshing beverage – whatever you're in the mood for. Find a table, grab something takeout and sit outside, or order from the menu. The daily specials are fantastic.

The Walk ≫ Bite is on the other side of the same block as Esker, with an indoor connector. Or you can go outside, turn back on 9th Ave SE toward Fort Calgary, and you'll see Esker on your left before the block is done.

ESKER FOUNDATION CONTEMPORARY ART GALLERY

The **Esker Foundation Contemporary Art Gallery** (https://eskerfoundation.com; 1011 9th Ave SE, Inglewood; ☺ 11am-6pm Sun, Tue & Wed, to 8pm Thu & Fri) is a great spot to duck into and enjoy the cool air con while you see the even cooler art that's on dis-

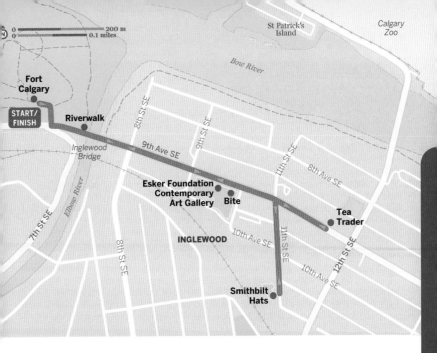

play. Thought-provoking, provocative, or just plain weird, there's always something to see here.

The Walk » From Esker, go back on 9th Ave SE and turn right onto 11th St. Smithbilt is a few blocks up on your right.

SMITHBILT HATS

Smithbilt Hats (☎403-244-9131; https:// smithbilthats.com; 1015 11th St SE; ⊙9am-5pm Mon-Wed & Fri, to 7pm Thu, 10am-4pm Sat) is the place to buy a hat. They run from 'cheap' (about $400) to jaw-dropping-what-the-hey prices (think $1300 or more!), but even if you just look, it's fascinating. The hats are pressed and cut to size right here. You can also see other styles (like top hats even Slash would envy!) and chat with the owners about anything hat you can think of.

The Walk » Exit and follow 11th St SE to 9th Ave, then turn right. The Tea Trader will be on the left, a small shop across from Dragon Pearl restaurant. It's easy to miss if you're not looking closely.

TEA TRADER

This lovely little **shop** (☎403-264-0728; www.teatrader.com; 1228a 9th Ave SE, Inglewood; ⊙10am-5pm Tue-Sat, noon-4pm Sun) has a delightful assortment of teas from around the world; while there's no tasting bar set up, you'll still 'taste' the magical aroma as you walk up the stairs. The staff are very friendly, and can guide you to your particular tea needs or to something fun and surprising you might not have tried before.

The Walk » Leave the shop, turn right and follow 9th Ave SE over Inglewood Bridge and back to your car at the parking lot.

BANFF & JASPER NATIONAL PARKS

With the Rocky Mountains stretched across them, Banff and Jasper National Parks are filled with dramatic, untamed wilderness. Rugged mountaintops scrape the skyline while enormous glaciers cling to their precipices. Glassy lakes flash emerald, turquoise and sapphire, filled by waterfalls tumbling down cliff faces and thundering through bottomless canyons. Deep forests blanket wide valleys and lofty alpine meadows explode with vibrant flowers. It's the scenery that you only expect to see on postcards, right here at your fingertips. And through it wander a cast of elusive wildlife characters such as bears, elk, moose, wolves and bighorn sheep.

Of the thousands of national parks scattered around the world today, Banff, created in 1885, is the third oldest and Canada's first, while adjacent Jasper was only 22 years behind. Situated on the eastern side of the Canadian Rockies, the two bordering parks were designated Unesco World Heritage sites in 1984. In contrast to some of North America's more remote parks, they both support small towns that lure from two to five million visitors each year.

Despite the throngs who come for the parks' more famous sites, like Lake Louise and Miette Hot Springs, it's by no means difficult to escape to a more tranquil experience of this sublime wonderland. However you choose to experience the parks, be it through hiking, backcountry skiing, paddling or simply sitting at a lake's edge beneath towering, castle-like mountains, the intensity and scale of these parks will bowl over even the most seasoned traveler. The more you see, the more you'll come to appreciate these parks' magic – and the more you'll want to discover.

Some of the best places to see the parks' charismatic large mammals are along remote roads like the Bow Valley Pkwy and the Icefields Pkwy – but you may also be lucky enough to see a bighorn, a bear or even a wolf right on the edge of town! No matter where you encounter them, it's crucial to respect the animals and give them space.

WILDLIFE CROSSINGS

As you drive north from Banff Town toward Lake Louise along the Trans-Canada Hwy/Hwy 1, look out for the six arched, tree-covered overpasses spanning the road. They're not for humans, but are actually wildlife crossings, which have been specially designed to allow Banff's animals to cross the road without fear of getting mowed down by a passing truck or recreational vehicle (RV).

Trans-Canada Hwy sits slap bang in the middle of several key 'wildlife corridors' (migratory routes between seasonal habitats) that crisscross the Bow Valley. Thousands of animals have been killed while trying to cross the highway over the years, especially since the road was widened to four lanes in 1981, and collisions with vehicles remain the number one cause of wildlife fatalities in the national park.

In order to reduce the risk of road accidents and protect the park's increasingly fragile animal population, the wildlife crossings were built at a cost of around C$1 million each starting in 1988, alongside 38 other underpasses that tunnel beneath the road at various points.

They seem to be working: according to Parks Canada, medium and large mammal fatalities dropped from 41 in 2006 to only 19 in 2015, and through 2016 more than a dozen animal species have used the crossings in excess of 165,000 times. Intriguingly, animals seem to have adapted to the crossings at different speeds: elk and deer began using them almost straight away, while it took as long as five years for warier species such as bears and wolves to adapt to them.

Different species also appear to have preferences for the types of bridges they like to use: elk, deer, moose, wolves and grizzly bears seem to like crossings that are high, wide and short, while black bears and cougars prefer them long, low and narrow.

A project is underway to monitor exactly which animals are using the crossings and how often, using DNA from barbed-wire fur traps positioned at the crossing entrances. Once the data has been collected and analyzed, additional crossings may be built near Lake Louise in coming years. Watch this space – or rather, watch this road.

Icefields Parkway

✔ 403, 780

Nothing in North America compares to the Icefields Parkway. For much of its 230km length, this ribbon of highway winding through the heart of the Canadian Rockies is the lone sign of human influence in an otherwise pristine wilderness of jewel-hued glacial lakes, unbroken virgin forest and otherworldly mountain crags.

Much of the route followed by the parkway was established over the millennia by indigenous people and later adopted by 19th-century fur traders. An early road was built during the 1930s as a Depression-era work project, and the present highway was opened in the early 1960s.

Nowadays it's used almost entirely by tourists, aside from the occasional elk, coyote or bighorn meandering along its perimeter. It can get busy in July and August, particularly with large recreational vehicles. Many also tackle it on a bike – the roadway is wide and sprinkled with plenty of strategically spaced campgrounds, hostels and lodges.

◉ Sights & Activities

There are two types of sights here: static (lakes, glaciers and mountains) and moving (elk, bears, moose etc). If you don't see at least one wild animal (look out for the inevitable 'bear jams') you'll be very unlucky.

★ **Athabasca Glacier**   GLACIER
See p37.

Mt Edith Cavell   MOUNTAIN
See p40.

Athabasca Falls   WATERFALL
See p39.

Columbia Icefield   GLACIER
About halfway between Lake Louise village and Jasper Town, you'll glimpse the vast Columbia Icefield, covering an area the size of Vancouver and feeding eight glaciers. This remnant of the last ice age is up to 350m thick in places and stretches across the plateau between Mt Columbia (3747m) and Mt Athabasca (3491m). For serious hikers and climbers, this is also the only accessible area of the icefield. For information and conditions, visit Parks Canada (p92) at the Columbia Icefield Discovery Centre.

This is the largest icefield in the Rockies, feeding the North Saskatchewan, Columbia, Athabasca, Mackenzie and Fraser River systems with its meltwaters. The mountainous sides of this vast bowl of ice are some of the highest in the Rockies, with nine peaks higher than 3000m.

Peyto Lake   LAKE
See p35.

Weeping Wall   WATERFALL
This imposing rock wall towers above the east side of the Icefields Parkway, a few kilometers south of Sunwapta Pass and the Banff–Jasper border. In summer it's a sea of waterfalls, with tears of liquid pouring from the top, creating a veil of moisture. Come winter, the water freezes up solid to form an enormous sheet of ice. The vertical ice field is a popular playground for ice climbers, who travel from around the globe to test their mettle here.

Wilcox Ridge   HIKING
See p36.

🛏 Sleeping & Eating

The Icefields Parkway is punctuated by several well-camouflaged hostels. Most are close to the highway in scenic locations. More substantial hotels/lodges are available at Bow Lake, Saskatchewan River Crossing, Columbia Icefield and Sunwapta Falls.

There are also numerous primitive campgrounds in the area, all of which are first-come, first-served.

Places to eat in these parts are extremely few and far between. By far the most atmospheric options are the dining rooms at the parkway's two historic lodges – Num-Ti-Jah, which was closed indefinitely at the time of writing, and Sunwapta (p92). Other than that you'll be stuck eating at the overpriced cafeteria-style restaurants at Saskatchewan River Crossing and the Icefield Discovery Centre. For picnic supplies or camping food, your best bet is to stock up in Jasper or Lake Louise.

Waterfowl
Lakes Campground   CAMPGROUND $
(Icefields Pkwy; tent & RV sites $21.50; ⊙ late Jun–early Sep) Tucked between two beautiful lakes about 60km north of Lake Louise, this campground just off the Icefields Pkwy has wooded sites and plenty of hiking opportunities. Facilities for the 116 first-come, first-served sites include flush toilets, hot water, BBQ shelters, food storage and interpretive

programs, but no showers. Sites 1, 2, 4, 6 and 10 are all near the lakeshore.

There is no cell coverage here, and there is an alcohol ban on long weekends.

HI Mt Edith Cavell
Wilderness Hostel
HOSTEL **$**

(☑ 780-852-3215; www.hihostels.ca; Cavell Rd; dm $38; ☺ reception 5-8pm mid-Feb–mid-Oct) 🏍 Secluded down a dead-end road near the base of Mt Edith Cavell and the Angel Glacier, this rustic place has wood-burning stoves in each of its two 16-bunk cabins and in the propane-lit kitchen-common room, where guests play cards and share stories of hikes to nearby Cavell Meadows and the remote Tonquin Valley (trailhead directly across the street).

There's no phone service, wi-fi, flush toilets or running water, but guests have use of showers at the main hostel in Jasper (p106). A manager runs the place from May to mid-October; in winter, the hostel is open for cross-country skiers on a key-collect system.

HI Mosquito Creek
Wilderness Hostel
HOSTEL **$**

(www.hihostels.ca; dm $38, private cabin for 2/3/4/5 people $95/115/135/155; ☺ reception 5-10pm, closed Oct & Tue Nov–Apr) Tucked away under the trees beside a rushing creek, this charming 34-bed backcountry hostel was originally built to house German POWs during WWII. There's a rustic wood-fired sauna, a stove-lit lounge and a pocket-sized

(propane-powered) kitchen where you can cook up communal grub. Two 12-bed dorms are supplemented by two private rooms sleeping up to five. No showers or electricity.

Sunwapta Falls
Rocky Mountain Lodge
HOTEL **$$$**

(☑ 780-852-4852; www.sunwapta.com; Icefields Pkwy; r $259-319; 🅿 @) A welcome Icefields rest stop 53km south of Jasper Town, Sunwapta offers a comfortable mix of suites and lodge rooms, each with a fireplace or wood-burning stove, all just a stone's throw from Sunwapta Falls. Clean and comfortable but not fancy, it's got a good restaurant on-site serving breakfast and dinner, and a cafeteria that's popular with the tour-bus crowd.

Glacier View Lodge
HOTEL **$$$**

(☑ 888-770-6914; www.banffjaspercollection.com; Icefield Centre, Icefields Pkwy; d with mountain/glacier view $489/519; ☺ mid-Apr–mid-Oct; 🅿 🛜) The panoramic perspectives over the glacier are unbelievable at this revamped hotel on the top floor of the Icefield Centre. Rooms have been given a total makeover, with loads of Scandinavian-style blonde wood, while the lobby area sports plush chairs and a telescope for admiring spectacular views through the floor-to-ceiling windows.

Sunwapta Falls
Rocky Mountain Lodge
CANADIAN **$$$**

(☑ 780-852-4852; www.sunwapta.com/restaurant; Icefields Pkwy; breakfast $12-18, dinner mains $25-43; ☺ 7-11am & 6-9pm May-Nov) With its stone fireplace, plank floors and white tablecloths, this roadside lodge's dining room makes an atmospheric spot for breakfast or dinner (just ignore that it's tucked in between a gift shop and a cafeteria). The locally driven menu features dishes like herb-crusted wild sockeye salmon, slow-roasted chicken with mashed potatoes, or beef and pork pot pie with maple-glazed root vegetables.

The adjacent deli serves breakfast, lunch and dinner cafeteria-style ($10 to $15).

ℹ Information

Columbia Icefield Discovery Centre (Icefields Pkwy) Situated on the Icefields Pkwy, close to the toe of the Athabasca Glacier, the green-roofed Icefield Centre is a bit of a zoo in the summer, with tour coaches cramming the car park. Decamp here to purchase tickets and board buses for the Snocoaches and Glacier Skywalk. You'll also find a hotel, cafeteria, restaurant, gift shop and Parks Canada infor-

Ice Explorer vehicle (p37), Athabasca Glacier
CHANTAL DE BRUIJNE/SHUTTERSTOCK ©

mation desk (☎780-852-6288; www.pc.gc.ca/pn-np/ab/jasper; Columbia Icefield Discovery Centre; ☉10:15am-5pm mid-May–Sep).

South Gate The entrance to the Parkway north of Lake Louise, where you can purchase your park pass and pick up a map and brochures.

Banff Town

☑403 / POP 7847

It seems hard to believe when you first lay eyes on Banff Town, but this overgrown village of less than 10,000 souls is the largest metropolis in the entire national park. Thankfully, Banff has largely avoided North America's notorious penchant for sprawl – though its few city blocks *do* manage to squeeze in a surprising amount of commercial hustle and bustle.

A resort town with boutique shops, nightclubs, museums and fancy restaurants may seem incongruous in this wild setting. But Banff is no ordinary town. It developed as a service center for the park that surrounds it. Today it brings in busloads of tourists keen to commune with shops as much as with nature; artists and writers are also drawn to the Rockies' unparalleled majesty. Whether you love or loathe Banff's cosmopolitan edge, wander 15 minutes in any direction and you're back in wild country, a primeval world of bears, elk and wolves.

◉ Sights

★**Banff National Park** NATIONAL PARK
See p19.

★**Whyte Museum of the Canadian Rockies** MUSEUM
(☎403-762-2291; www.whyte.org; 111 Bear St; adult/student/child $10/5/free; ☉10am-5pm) Founded by local artists Catharine and Peter Whyte, the century-old Whyte Museum is more than just a rainy-day option. It boasts a beautiful, ever-changing gallery displaying art from 1800 to the present, by regional, Canadian and international artists, many with a focus on the Rockies. Watch for work by the Group of Seven (aka the Algonquin School). There's also a permanent collection telling the story of Banff and the hardy men and women who forged a home among the mountains.

Attached to the museum is an archive with thousands of photographs spanning the history of the town and park; these are available for reprint. The museum also organizes guided walking tours focused on Banff's history ($20) and heritage homes ($10).

Upper Hot Springs Pool HOT SPRINGS
(www.hotsprings.ca; Mountain Ave; adult/child/family $8.30/6.30/24.50; ☉9am-11pm mid-May–mid-Oct, 10am-10pm Sun-Thu, to 11pm Fri & Sat rest of year) Banff quite literally wouldn't be Banff if it weren't for its hot springs, which gush out from 2.5km beneath Sulphur Mountain at a constant temperature of between 32°C (90°F) and 46°C (116°F) – it was the springs that drew the first tourists to Banff. You can still sample the soothing mineral waters here, near the Banff Gondola.

Several hotels once occupied the site where the present-day Upper Hot Springs Pool stands – Dr RG Brett's Grand View Villa, built in 1886, was joined by the Hydro Hotel in 1890, but both establishments burnt down and were replaced in the 1930s by a fashionable art-deco style.

Renovations have since masked some of the bathhouse's period elegance, but the hot springs still rank as one of the not-to-be-missed Banff experiences – there aren't many places in the world where you can take a hot bath with a mountain view as spectacular as this.

The pools get busy in season, so aim for an early or late dip if you prefer smaller crowds (alternatively, with three weeks' advance notice you can hire the whole place for $270 per hour). Towels and swimsuits are available for hire.

Fairmont Banff Springs HISTORIC BUILDING
(www.fairmont.com/banffsprings; 405 Spray Ave) Looming up beside the Bow River, the Banff Springs is a local landmark in more ways than one. Originally built in 1888, and remodeled in 1928 to resemble a cross between a Scottish baronial castle and a European château, the turret-topped exterior conceals

> ## FILM & BOOK FEST
>
> The highlight of Banff's annual cultural calendar, Banff Mountain Film & Book Festival (www.banffcentre.ca/banff-mountain-film-book-festival; ☉Oct-Nov) is a nine-day festival in late October and early November. Attracting the cream of the mountain-culture crop, it's packed with film screenings and book readings for the armchair adventurer and mountain guru alike. Many events take place at the Banff Centre's Eric Harvie Theatre.

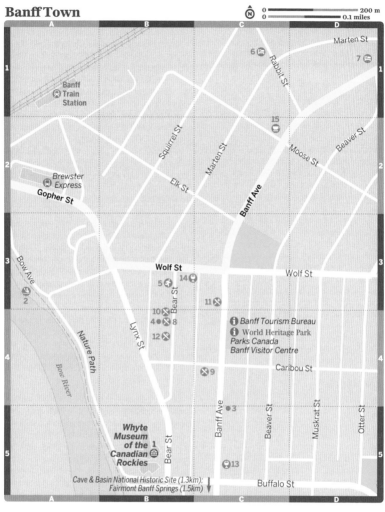

an eye-poppingly extravagant selection of ballrooms, lounges, dining rooms and balustraded staircases that would make William Randolph Hearst green with envy.

Highlights include an Arthurian great hall; an elegant, wood-paneled bar; and the gorgeous hot-springs spa. Even if you're not staying here, you're welcome to wander around, and it's worth splashing out on a coffee, a meal or a cocktail in one of the hotel's dozen or so restaurants, lounges and bars.

The hotel is best seen in winter, when the lights of its 700-odd rooms twinkle out from under a thick crust of snow.

Cave & Basin
National Historic Site   HISTORIC SITE
(☎403-762-1566; www.pc.gc.ca/en/lhn-nhs/ab/caveandbasin; 311 Cave Ave; adult/child $3.90/free; ⓣ9:30am-5pm mid-May–mid-Oct, 11am-5pm Wed-Sun rest of year) The Canadian National Park system was effectively born at these hot springs, discovered accidentally by three Canadian Pacific Railway employees on their day off in 1883 (though known to indigenous peoples for 10,000 years). The springs quickly spurred a flurry of private businesses offering facilities for bathers to enjoy the then-trendy thermal treatments. To avert an environmental catastrophe, the government

Banff Town

🏅 Top Sights

🏆 Activities, Courses & Tours

🛏 Sleeping

🍴 Eating

🍷 Drinking & Nightlife

stepped in, declaring Banff Canada's first national park in order to preserve the springs.

There's no swimming here anymore, but visitors can see the original cave, then stroll out onto a terrace that covers the former lower mineral springs pool. From here, a boardwalk with interpretive signage leads uphill to additional springs and the cave's upper vent.

Signposted just behind the complex are two more walking trails: the 2.3km Marsh Loop Trail across the park's only natural river marsh, and the Sundance Canyon Trail, leading along the Bow River to a beautiful side canyon.

🏃 Activities

Canoeing & Kayaking

Despite a modern penchant for big cars, canoe travel is still very much a quintessential Canadian method of transportation. The best options near Banff Town are Lake Minnewanka and nearby Two Jack Lake, both to the northeast, or – closer to the town itself – the Vermilion Lakes. Unless you have your own canoe, you'll need to rent one; try Banff Canoe Club (📞403-762-5005; www.banffcanoeclub.com; cnr Wolf St & Bow Ave; canoe & kayak rental per 1st/additional hour $45/25, SUP/bike rental per hour $30/12; ⊙9am-9pm mid-Jun–Aug, reduced hours mid-May–mid-Jun & Sep).

Cycling

There are lots of riding options around Banff, both on the road and on selected trails. Popular routes around Banff Town include Sundance (7.4km round-trip) and Spray River Loop (12.5km); either is good for families. Spray River & Goat Creek (19km one way) and Rundle Riverside (14km one way) are both A-to-Bs with start/finish points near Canmore. The former is pretty straightforward; the latter is more challenging, with ups and downs and potential for thrills and spills.

Serious road cyclists should check out Hwy 1A (the Bow Valley Pkwy) between Banff and Lake Louise; the rolling hills and quiet road here are a roadie's dream. Parks Canada publishes the brochure *Mountain Biking & Cycling Guide – Banff National Park,* which describes trails and regulations. Pick it up at the Banff Visitor Centre (p100).

Snowtips/Bactrax (📞403-762-8177; www.snowtips-bactrax.com; 225 Bear St; bike rental per hour/day from $10/35, cross-country/alpine ski rental per day from $20/40; ⊙8am-8pm Jun–mid-Oct, 7am-9pm rest of year) has a barn full of town and trail bikes to rent and will deliver them to your hotel.

Hiking

Hiking is Banff's key attraction and therefore the focus of many travelers who visit the area. The trails are easy to find, well signposted and maintained enough to be comfortable to walk on, yet rugged enough to provide a wilderness experience.

In general, the closer to Banff Town you are, the more people you can expect to see and the more developed the trail will be. But regardless of where in the park you go walking, you are assured to be rewarded for your efforts.

Before you head out, check at the Banff Visitor Centre (p100) for trail conditions and possible closures. Keep in mind that trails are often snow-covered much later into the summer season than you might expect, and trail closures due to bears are a possibility, especially in berry season (July to September).

One of the best hikes from the town center is the Bow River Falls & The Hoodoos Trail, which starts by the Bow River Bridge and tracks past the falls to the Hoodoos – weird-looking rock spires caused by wind and water erosion. The trail works its way around the back of Tunnel Mountain through forest and some river meadows (10.2km round-trip).

Rafting on Kananaskis River
JAMES_GABBERT/GETTY IMAGES ©

You can track the north shore of Lake Minnewanka for kilometers on a multi-use trail that is sometimes closed due to bear activity. The classic hike is to walk as far as the Aylmer Lookout, nearly 12km one way. Less taxing is the 5.6km round-trip hike to Stewart Canyon, where you can clamber down rocks and boulders to the Cascade River.

Some of the best multiday hikes start at the Sunshine Village parking lot (where skiers grab the gondola in winter). From here you can plan two- to four-day sorties up over Healy Pass and down to Egypt Lake, or else catch the gondola up to Sunshine Village (p96), where you can cross the border into BC and head out across Sunshine Meadows into Mt Assiniboine Provincial Park.

The best backcountry experience is arguably the Sawback Trail, which travels from Banff up to Lake Louise the back way – it's over 74km, with six primitive campsites and three spectacular mountain passes.

Check out Lonely Planet's *Banff, Jasper & Glacier National Parks* guide for more details about more single-day and multiday hikes.

Horseback Riding

Banff's first European explorers – fur traders and railway engineers – penetrated the region primarily on horseback. You can recreate their pioneering spirit on guided rides with Banff Trail Riders (☑ 403-762-

4551; www.horseback.com; 138 Banff Ave; guided rides per person $64-196), which will fit you out with a trusty steed and lead you on a one- to three-hour day trip or bring you into the backcountry for an overnight adventure at its Sundance Lodge. Instruction and guiding are included; a sore backside is more or less mandatory for beginners. Grin and bear it.

Skiing & Snowboarding

There are three ski areas in the national park, two of them in the vicinity of Banff Town. Large, snowy Sunshine Village is considered world-class. Tiny Norquay, a mere 5km from the center, is your half-day, family-friendly option.

Sunshine Village (www.skibanff.com; day ski pass adult/youth $114/89) straddles the Alberta–BC border. Though slightly smaller than Lake Louise in terms of skiable terrain, it gets much bigger dumpings of snow, or 'Champagne powder' as Albertans like to call it (up to 9m annually). Aficionados laud Sunshine's advanced runs and lengthy ski season, which lingers until Victoria Day weekend in late May. A high-speed gondola whisks skiers up in 17 minutes to the village, which sports Banff's only ski-in hotel, the Sunshine Mountain Lodge.

Mt Norquay (☑ 403-762-4421; www.banff-norquay.com; Mt Norquay Rd; day ski pass adult/youth/child $89/68/35; ⊙ 9am-4pm; ⊞), a short distance uphill from downtown Banff, has a long history of entertaining Banff visitors. The smallest and least visited of the three local hills, this is a good place to body-swerve the major show-offs and hit the slopes for a succinct half-day.

Local buses shuttle riders from Banff hotels to both resorts (and Lake Louise) every 30 minutes during the season.

White-Water Rafting

The best rafting is outside the park (and province) on the Kicking Horse River in Yoho National Park, BC. There are Class IV rapids here, meaning big waves, swirling holes and a guaranteed soaking. Lesser rapids are found on the Kananaskis River and the Horseshoe Canyon section of the Bow River. The Bow River around Banff is better suited to mellower float trips.

Several rafting companies are located in the park, including Hydra River Guides (p97) and Rocky Mountain Raft Tours (☑ 403-762-3632; www.banffrafttours.com; Golf Course Loop Rd; ⊙ mid-May–late Sep; ⊞). Tour prices start around $60 for a one-hour float.

Tours

Via Ferrata

OUTDOORS

(☑844-667-7829; www.banffnorquay.com/summer/via-ferrata; Mt Norquay; ⊘mid-Jun–mid-Oct) These fixed-protection climbing routes on Mt Norquay let your test your head for heights. Choose from the Explorer ($169, 2½ hours), the Ridgewalker ($219, four hours), the Skyline ($279, five hours) and the Summiteer ($349, six hours), which includes a three-wire suspension bridge to the top of Mt Norquay. Prices include full safety kit, accompanying guide and passage up the Norquay chairlift to the start point.

Hydra River Guides

RAFTING

(☑403-762-4554; www.raftbanff.com; 211 Bear St; ⊘7:30am-9pm) This well-regarded company has been running rafting trips for over three decades. The most popular is the 20km Kicking Horse Classic ($149), with varied rapids (up to class IV) and a BBQ lunch; novices and families will appreciate the sedate Mild float trip (adult/child $79/59); for late risers there's the Last Waltz ($115), which doesn't get going until midafternoon. Hydra also offers combo packages including horseback riding, zip-lining and ATV driving.

Sleeping

Accommodations in Banff Town are generally expensive, especially in summer. Booking ahead is strongly recommended.

For listings of available accommodations, check the Banff Tourism Bureau (p100) and the Parks Canada Visitor Centre (p100).

Parks Canada operates several popular campgrounds. Sites at Tunnel Mountain and Two Jack – the two closest to town – should be reserved months in advance; others along the Bow Valley Parkway/Hwy 1A are first-come, first-served.

★ Samesun Banff

HOSTEL $

(☑403-762-4499; www.banffhostel.com; 433 Banff Ave; dm incl breakfast from $65; P @ 🛜) Catering to a youthful international backpacker crowd, the welcoming Samesun offers a central Banff Ave location, a full lineup of daily activities (hiking, cycling, canoeing, hot springs) and 112 dorm beds spread across modern, compact six- to 14-person rooms (some with fireplaces). A DIY breakfast is included, and the bustling on-site Beaver resto-bar keeps everyone happy with nightly drink specials.

THE MOUNTAIN MAN

Driving into Banff you might notice a distinctive face staring at you from the town-limits sign, sporting a jaunty hat, a drooping meerschaum pipe and a rather splendid handlebar moustache. Meet 'Wild' Bill Peyto, one of the great characters of the Canadian Rockies and the original wild man of the mountains.

Born in Kent, England, in 1869, Bill was the third eldest of a family of nine children. Having left the cramped environs of the Peyto household at 17, he set out for Canada, arriving in Halifax in 1887, where he initially found work as a railway laborer, part-time rancher and government employee. But it wasn't long before Bill found his true calling – as a mountain guide working for the packing and outfitting business owned by Tom Wilson.

Over the next decade he proved himself a skilled trapper, hunter and alpinist, exploring Mistaya Valley and Peyto Lake, making the first successful ascent of Bow Summit in 1894 and notching up the first (failed) attempt at Mt Assiniboine the following year (he eventually scaled it in 1902). He even found time for some book-larnin', schooling himself in paleontology and geology using secondhand textbooks. Within a matter of years he had become one of the most skilled amateur naturalists in the Rockies.

He was also a notorious showman with an eye for a natty outfit. One of his clients, Norman Collie, painted a vivid picture of Wild Bill: 'Peyto assumes a wild and picturesque though somewhat tattered attire. A sombrero, with a rakish tilt to one side, a blue shirt set off by a white kerchief (which may have served civilization for napkin), and a buckskin coat with a fringe border add to his cowboy appearance. A heavy belt containing a row of cartridges, hunting knife and six-shooter as well as the restless activity of his wicked blue eyes, give him an air of bravado...'

You can still visit one of Bill's original log cabins on the grounds of the Whyte Museum in Banff, and his action-packed diary – which is appropriately titled *Ain't It Hell: Bill Peyto's Mountain Journal* – is available from the museum shop.

Two Jack Lakeside
CAMPGROUND $

(Minnewanka Loop Dr; tent & RV sites $27.40; ⊙ May-Oct; P) Right on Two Jack Lake, 11km northeast of town, Two Jack Lakeside is the most scenic of the Banff-area campgrounds, usually filling its 74 reservable sites months in advance. You can now also 'glamp' at Two Jack in one of 10 'oTENTiks' – fully serviced A-frame 'tents' with hot showers and electricity, sleeping up to six people for $120 per night.

★ Buffaloberry
B&B $$$

(✎ 403-762-3750; www.buffaloberry.com; 417 Marten St; r $465; P ❋ ☎) Centrally located and surrounded by colorful flowering plants, this purpose-built B&B makes a cheerful, comfortable home base. The four individually decorated bedrooms are heavy on homey charm, and the underfloor heating and nightly turn-down treats keep the pamper factor high. With an ever-changing menu (think baked Camembert egg custard or 'triple B' – blueberry, buttermilk and buckwheat – pancakes), breakfasts are divine.

★ Fairmont Banff Springs
HOTEL $$$

(✎ 403-762-2211; www.fairmont.com/banff-springs; 405 Spray Ave; r from $599; P ❋ @ ☎ ✉) Rising like a Gaelic Balmoral above the trees at the base of Sulphur Mountain and visible from miles away, the Banff Springs is a wonder of early 1920s revivalist architecture and one of Canada's most iconic buildings. Wandering through its grand lobby and elegant lounge, wine bar and restaurant, it's easy to forget that it's also a hotel.

Rooms vary in size and style; some don't feel much different than a standard hotel room, while others have plush modern or old-world decor. Many have incredible views. Service and prices are fit for royalty.

✕ Eating

Banff dining is more than just hiker food. There's a wide range of international cuisine represented along Banff Ave and Bear St, and some of the more elegant places will inspire grubby hikers to return to their hotel shower before pulling up a chair. Many Banff hotels also welcome nonguests to excellent on-site restaurants. AAA Alberta beef features on most menus, while veggie, vegan and gluten-free alternatives are increasingly available.

Wild Flour
CAFE $

(✎ 403-760-5074; www.wildflourbakery.ca; 211 Bear St; mains $5-10; ⊙ 7am-4pm; ☎ ✎) ✎ If you're searching for an inexpensive snack or a relatively guilt-free sugary treat, make a beeline for Banff's best bakery, where you'll find cheesecake, dark-chocolate torte and macaroons – along with breakfasts, delicious fresh-baked focaccia, well-stuffed sandwiches on homemade bread, and soups, all of it organic. Not surprisingly, the place gets busy – but outdoor courtyard seating helps alleviate the crush.

VIEWFINDER/SHUTTERSTOCK ©

Banff Avenue at twilight

BOW VALLEY PARKWAY

While most people zoom along busy Trans-Canada Hwy/Hwy 1 with nothing but views of truck tailgates and passing automobiles, wiser souls swing over onto the quieter and much more scenic Hwy 1A, otherwise known as the Bow Valley Pkwy, which runs for 51km (31.6 miles) nearly all the way north to Lake Louise. The route is hemmed in by thick fir forest and mountains, with regular viewpoints looking out across the Bow Valley. It's a great place to look out for wildlife, especially elk, bighorn sheep and even the occasional moose, but take things slow: the regular speed limit is 60km/h (37mph), dropping down to 30km/h (19mph) at certain sections to avoid wildlife collisions.

If you're short on time, at the very least make sure to visit the thundering waterfalls of **Johnston Canyon**, where a suspended catwalk tracks along the canyon wall to a series of viewpoints overlooking the Lower and Upper Falls. It's one of Banff's most popular sights, and the car park is often full by midmorning; save it for an early morning or late-evening visit. A little further along the parkway is the lookout point at Castle Mountain, one of Banff's most recognizable mountain peaks.

The eastern section of the road between Fireside Picnic Area and Johnston Canyon is closed from 6pm to 9am during spring mating season (March to late June).

★ **Eddie Burger Bar**   BURGERS $$
(☑ 403-762-2230; www.eddieburgerbar.ca; 6/137 Banff Ave; burgers $17-23; ⊙ 11am-2am, from 11:30am Oct-May) Not your average fast-food joint, Eddie's is devoted to building large, custom-made and crave-worthy burgers, from the usual classics to specialties like the elk burger with blueberry chutney. Add to this a hearty helping of poutine and an Oreo milkshake or a shaken Caesar (cocktail, not salad!) garnished with a chicken wing, and you're set – for the next week.

Thankfully its easy to get comfortable in this diner-style sports bar, and (blessedly!) they keep the kitchen open late (till 1:30am) to satisfy cases of the late-night munchies.

★ **Bear Street Tavern**   PUB FOOD $$
(☑ 403-762-2021; www.bearstreettavern.ca; 211 Bear St; mains $15-25; ⊙ 11:30am-late) This gastropub hits a double whammy: ingeniously flavored pizzas washed down with locally brewed pints. Banffites head here in droves for a plate of pulled-pork nachos or a bison-and-onion pizza, accompanied by pitchers of hoppy ale. The patio overlooking Bison Courtyard is the best place to linger if the weather cooperates.

Nourish   VEGETARIAN $$
(☑ 403-760-3933; www.nourishbistro.com; 211 Bear St; mains $18-26; ⊙ 11:30am-10:30pm Mon-Thu, 7:30-10:30am & 11:30am-10:30pm Fri-Sun; 🖋) Confronted by a strangely beautiful papier-mâché tree when you walk in the door, you instantly know this vegetarian bistro is not average. With locally sourced dishes like wild-

mushroom ravioli, Moroccan cauliflower bites or 27-ingredient nachos with Canadian cheddar or vegan queso, Nourish has carved out a gourmet following in Banff. Dinner is served as shareable tapas and larger plates.

It seems amiss to not mention the three-column drinks list (beer, cider and creative cocktails) and the funky tables made from Bow River wood.

Juniper Bistro   BISTRO $$$
(☑ 403-763-6219; www.thejuniper.com/dining; 1 Juniper Way; breakfast & small plates from $14, mains $28-34; ⊙ 7am-11pm; 🖋) Spectacular mountain views combine with an innovative, locally sourced menu at Juniper's, a surprisingly good hotel restaurant on Banff's northern outskirts. Beyond breakfasts and dinners, the midafternoon 'Graze' menu is also enticing – think small plates of orange and cardamom-poached beets or bison carpaccio with juniper berry and pink peppercorn, all accompanied by fab cocktails and 'mocktails'. Vegetarian, vegan and gluten-free options abound.

Park   AMERICAN $$$
(☑ 403-762-5114; www.parkdistillery.com; 219 Banff Ave; mains $19-52; ⊙ 11am-10pm) Banff gets hip with a microdistillery to complement its microbrewery, plying spirits (gin, vodka and whiskey) and beer made from Alberta's foothills' grain. It all goes down perfectly with a mesquite beef hoagie, fish tacos or anything off the excellent appetizer menu. Cocktails are creative, fun and ever-changing.

🍷 Drinking & Nightlife

Throw a stone on Banff Ave and you're more likely to hit a gap-year traveler than a local. This makes for a lively, if rather young, drinking scene. Many of the local watering holes also have live music. Have a look through the entertainment listings at Banff Crag & Canyon (www.thecragandcanyon.ca).

★ **Grapes** WINE BAR
(📞 403-762-6860; www.fairmont.com/banff-springs/dining/grapeswinebar; Fairmont Banff Springs, 405 Spray Ave; 5-9:30pm Sun-Thu, from 3pm Fri & Sat) Sporting original crown molding and dark wood paneling from its early days as a ladies' writing salon, this intimate wine bar in Banff's Fairmont makes an elegant spot for afternoon aperitifs. British Columbian Meritage and Ontario Riesling share the menu with international vintages, while tapas of house-cured meats, cheeses, pickled veggies and candied steelhead will tempt you to linger for dinner.

Whitebark Cafe COFFEE
(📞 403-760-7298; www.whitebarkcafe.com; 401 Banff Ave; 6:30am-7pm) Early risers in need of their java fix should head straight to this sleek corner cafe attached to the Aspen Lodge. It's renowned among locals not only for its superb coffee, but also for its muffins, snacks and sandwiches. For an unconventional (and inexpensive) breakfast, check out its bacon-and-egg breakfast cup, a mini-meal encased in delicious flaky pastry.

Banff Ave Brewing Co MICROBREWERY
(📞 403-762-1003; www.banffavebrewingco.ca; 110 Banff Ave; 11am-2am) Banff Ave's sprawling 2nd-floor beer hall bustles day and night, slinging a dozen craft brews created on the premises alongside a wide range of nibbles: buttered soft pretzels, bratwurst, burgers and the like. Late-night half-price pizza specials offer welcome relief to late-returning hikers and help keep things hopping into the wee hours.

St James's Gate Olde Irish Pub PUB
(📞 403-762-9355; www.stjamesgatebanff.com; 207 Wolf St; 11am-2am) Banff is a Celtic name, so it's hardly surprising to find an Irish pub here, and a rather good one at that. Check out the woodwork, crafted and shipped from the old country. Aside from stout on tap and a healthy selection of malts, there's classic pub grub, including an epic steak-and-Guinness pie.

ℹ️ Information

Banff Tourism Bureau (📞 403-762-8421; www.banfflakelouise.com; 224 Banff Ave; 8am-8pm mid-May–Sep, 9am-5pm rest of year) Opposite the Parks Canada desks in the Banff Visitor Centre, this info desk provides advice on accommodations, activities and attractions.

Parks Canada Banff Visitor Centre (📞 403-762-1550; www.pc.gc.ca/banff; 224 Banff Ave; 8am-8pm mid-May–Sep, 9am-5pm rest of year) The Parks Canada office provides park info and maps. This is where you can find current trail conditions and weather forecasts, and register for backcountry hiking and camping.

Lake Louise

📞 403 / POP 1175

Famous for its teahouses, grizzly bears and hiking trails, Lake Louise is also renowned for its much-commented-on 'crowds,' plus the incongruous lump of towering concrete known as Chateau Lake Louise. But frankly, who cares? You don't come to Lake Louise to dodge other tourists. You come to share in one of the Rockies' most spectacular sights, one that has captured the imaginations of mountaineers, artists and visitors for more than a century.

Despite the tourist throngs and the endless hype, there are plenty of places where you can still appreciate Lake Louise on your own terms. Ultimately, it's just as simple as finding your own nook and settling down to contemplate the sublime scenery. When you're done with gawping, romancing or pledging undying love to your partner on the shimmering lakeshore, try hiking up into the mountainous landscape behind, or walking back down to the village along the pleasantly wooded Louise Creek trail.

Lake Louise 'village,' just off Trans-Canada Hwy/Hwy 1, is little more than an outdoor shopping mall, a gas station and a handful of hotels.

◎ Sights

★ **Lake Louise** LAKE
See p20

★ **Moraine Lake** LAKE
See p20

Morant's Curve Viewpoint VIEWPOINT
Evoking oohs, ahs and countless shutter clicks from every traveler who passes near, this pullover and viewpoint on the Bow Val-

ley Pkwy/Hwy 1A sits at a scenic curve in the Bow River much favored by both the Canadian Pacific Railway and *National Geographic* photographer Nicholas Morant (1910–99), whose images helped publicize Banff during its early days as a national park.

Lake Louise Summer Gondola   CABLE CAR
(📞403-522-3555; www.lakelouisegondola.com; 1 Whitehorn Rd; adult/child $38/17; ⊙9am-4pm mid-May–mid-Jun, 8am-5:30pm mid-Jun–Jul, to 6pm Aug, to 5pm Sep–mid-Oct; 👪) For a bird's-eye view of the Lake Louise area – and a good chance of spotting grizzly bears on the avalanche slopes – climb aboard the Lake Louise Gondola, which crawls up the side of Whitehorn Mountain via an open ski lift or enclosed gondola to a dizzying viewpoint 2088m above the valley floor. Look out for the imposing fang of 3544m-high Mt Temple piercing the skyline on the opposite side of the valley.

🏃 Activities

Once you've gawped at the shimmering lake, hike into the beckoning mountains beyond. Lake Louise also has a lauded ski resort and enticing cross-country options. To the southeast, 13km along a winding seasonal road, is spectacular Moraine Lake and its equally beguiling backdrop. In summer, this narrow road is periodically shut to new visitors to empty out the traffic.

★ Lake Agnes & the Beehives   HIKING
Two compelling attractions make this Lake Louise's most popular hike. First, the historic Lake Agnes Teahouse (p102), where hikers have been refueling since 1901, makes a supremely atmospheric spot to break for tea, sandwiches and baked goods at the 3.4km mark. Second, the lake views from atop 2270m Big Beehive (the trail's ultimate destination) are phenomenal. Set off early to beat the crowds.

★ Skoki Valley Trail   WALKING
The beautiful multiday hike into Skoki Valley is one of Banff's classic backcountry adventures. Starting from Temple Lodge at Lake Louise ski resort, the trail leads over Boulder Pass and Deception Pass, past numerous lakes and around Fossil Mountain to the rustic 1930s-vintage Skoki Lodge (p102) and Merlin Meadows wilderness campground. From here, various loop hikes fan out into the wilderness.

Lake Louise Ski Resort   SKIING
(📞403-522-3555; www.skilouise.com; 1 Whitehorn Rd; day pass adult/youth $114/98; 👪) Lake Louise is the largest of Banff's 'Big Three' resorts (the other two being Sunshine and Norquay). It offers a humongous 1700 hectares of skiable land divided between 145 runs. It's great for families, with a good spread of beginner-rated (25%) runs on the Front Side/South Face (especially

---

❶ HIKING RESTRICTIONS AROUND LAKE LOUISE

The Lake Louise area is one of three key grizzly-bear habitats in Banff National Park, and supports a number of grizzly sows and their cubs. To avoid bear encounters, park authorities often impose access restrictions in summer on several trails around Lake Louise, including the Consolation Lakes Trail, Larch Valley, Sentinel Pass, Paradise Valley and Wenkchemna Pass.

Under the rules, hikers are required by law to travel in tight groups of at least four people, and take the usual precautions to avoid bear encounters (make noise on the trail, carry bear spray etc). Other routes (including the Moraine Lake Highline Trail) may also be closed according to bear activity – check ahead with park staff. If you're caught breaching the 'group of four' rule, you'll be up for a hefty fine, so stick to the rules: they're there for your own safety.

The timetable varies every year according to bear activity and the berry season, but usually begins around mid-July and lasts until early September. Restrictions are clearly posted in park offices and at trailheads.

If your group is short, the Lake Louise Visitor Centre keeps a logbook where you can leave your details to get in touch with other hikers to make up the required numbers. Alternatively, leave your details at one of the local hostels or just hang around the trailheads at the start of the day – you're bound to find another group who won't mind you tagging along.

around the base area), along with plenty of intermediate-rated (45%) runs. The longest (8km) is on the Larch Face.

Lake Louise has plenty of powder and off-piste skiing for advanced skiers, too, as well as a snowboard park and tube rides. However, its average snowfall is only around half that of Sunshine Village, meaning that snow machines are often used to supplement the natural snowpack.

🛏 Sleeping

Other than a very popular hostel and a fantastic riverside campground, Lake Louise doesn't have much in the way of budget accommodations. At the pricier end of the spectrum you'll find some truly splurge-worthy properties, including cabins, historic lodges and two of the Canadian Rockies' most iconic lakeside hotels.

★ Skoki Lodge   LODGE $$

(☑ 403-522-3555; www.skoki.com; r per person incl 3 meals & afternoon tea $240-305) Built in 1931 and overlooking a glorious high mountain valley, Skoki was one of the Canadian Rockies' earliest backcountry lodges and remains one of the most magical places to stay in the whole national park. The rustic but delightfully cozy lodge is only accessible on foot, horseback or skis via an 11km climb over two high mountain passes from Lake Louise.

Lake Louise Tent & RV Campground   CAMPGROUND $

(www.reservation.pc.gc.ca; Lake Louise village; tent/RV sites $27.40/32.30; ⊙tent park Jun-Sep, RV park year-round) Near the village, this efficient, wooded 395-site campground accommodates RVs on one side of the river and tents and soft-sided vehicles on the other, protected from bears behind an electric fence. Choose a site away from the railway tracks to enjoy views of Mt Temple in relative peace. Book online through the Parks Canada website.

HI Lake Louise Alpine Centre   HOSTEL $

(☑ 403-522-2201; www.hihostels.ca; 203 Village Rd, Lake Louise village; dm/d $64/192; P) This is what a hostel should be – clean, friendly and full of interesting travelers – and the rustic, comfortable lodge-style buildings, with plenty of raw timber and stone, are fine examples of Canadian Rockies architecture. Dorm rooms are fairly standard and the small private rooms are a bit overpriced, but this is as close as you'll get to budget in Lake Louise.

★ Moraine Lake Lodge   HOTEL $$$

(☑ 403-522-3733; www.morainelakelodge.com; 1 Moraine Lake Rd; r/cabin from $717/964; ⊙ Jun-Sep; P 🐾) 🦮 The experience here is intimate, personal and private, and the service is famously good. While billed as rustic (ie no TVs), the rooms and cabins offer mountain-inspired luxury with big picture windows, wood-burning or antique gas fireplaces, soaking tubs, feather comforters and balconies overlooking the lake. The fine-dining restaurant on-site wins equal plaudits. Canoe use is free for guests.

★ Paradise Lodge & Bungalows   CABIN $$$

(☑ 403-522-3595; www.paradiselodge.com; Lake Louise Dr; cabins $345-488, r in lodge $415-475; ⊙mid-May–Sep) These cozy, lovingly restored 1930s log cabins along the Lake Louise road are only moments from the lakeshore. Each is unique, but expect comfy beds, kitchens or kitchenettes and claw-foot soaking tubs. Newer lodge rooms are hotel-style. Cheerful flowery grounds and tree-shaded lawns provide ample lounging opportunities. Kids will love the playground and miniature doghouse cabin for Beau the pooch.

★ Deer Lodge   HOTEL $$$

(☑ 403-410-7417; www.crmr.com; 109 Lake Louise Dr; r from $329; P 🐾) Tucked demurely behind Chateau Lake Louise, historic Deer Lodge dates from the 1920s and has managed to keep its genuine alpine feel intact. The rustic exterior and maze of corridors can't have changed much since the days of bobbed hair and F Scott Fitzgerald. Lodge rooms are fairly small but quaint, while spacious Heritage rooms have smart, boutique-like furnishings.

🍴 Eating & Drinking

For its size, Lake Louise has a surprisingly decent selection of places at which to fill your belly. Most are concentrated up near the lake or down in Lake Louise village between Samson Mall and the train station.

★ Lake Agnes Teahouse   TEAHOUSE $

(www.lakeagnesteahouse.com; lunch $7.50-15; ⊙8am-5pm early Jun-early Oct) The 3.4km hike from Lake Louise to Lake Agnes is among the area's most popular – surely because it ends here. This fabulously rustic alpine teahouse perched at 2135m (7005ft) seems to hang in the clouds beside the ethereal lake and its adjacent waterfall. Homemade soup, thick-cut sandwiches and lake-water tea help fuel the jaunt back down. Cash only. Expect queues.

Skoki Lodge

Trailhead Café SANDWICHES $

(📞403-522-2006; www.facebook.com/lakelouiseAB; Samson Mall, Lake Louise village; sandwiches $6-10; ⊗7am-6pm) This is *the* place to come for breakfast or a takeout lunch. Wraps and sandwiches are made to order, the staff are well versed in the espresso machine, and the omelets, buttermilk pancakes and lox cream-cheese bagels will fuel you for the trail without breaking the bank. Expect a queue.

Plain of Six Glaciers Teahouse TEAHOUSE $$

(snacks & meals $9.50-25; ⊗9am-5pm mid-Jun–early Oct) Constructed in 1927 as a way station for Swiss mountaineering guides leading clients up to the summit of Mt Victoria, this twin-level log chalet looks like something out of the pages of *Heidi*. Nestled in a quiet glade at 2100m, it dishes up homemade sandwiches, cakes, gourmet teas and hot chocolates to a steady stream of puffed-out hikers.

★Lake Louise Station Restaurant CANADIAN $$$

(📞403-522-2600; www.lakelouisestation.com; 200 Sentinel Rd, Lake Louise village; mains lunch $16-26, dinner $20-48; ⊗11:30am-4pm & 5-9pm Jun-Sep, noon-4pm & 5-8:30pm Wed-Sun Oct-May) Lake Louise's historic train station is the most atmospheric place in town to have a meal. Details like stacks of turn-of-the-century luggage, the stationmaster's desk and the original dining cars out back transport you back to 1910, when the elegant edifice was first built. Dig into maple-glazed salmon, Wiener schnitzel

or slow-braised bison ribs and soak up the vintage vibe. Reservations recommended.

Bill Peyto's Café CAFE $$

(📞403-522-2201; www.hihostels.ca/en/about/hostels/bill-peytos-cafe; HI-Lake Louise Alpine Centre, Village Rd; mains breakfast $11-14, lunch & dinner $14-19; ⊗7am-10pm May-Sep, 7.30am-9:30pm Oct-Apr) This hostel-administered resto-pub draws a casual, budget-minded crowd for its reasonably priced food and good draft beer. Fill up on homemade granola or bacon and eggs at breakfast; go for burgers, pasta, battered cod and chips, or mac 'n' cheese at dinner. The patio is nice when the sun (or moon) is shining. Expect queues when the hostel's full.

ℹ️ Information

Lake Louise Backcountry Trails Office

(📞403-522-1264; Lake Louise Visitor Centre, Lake Louise village; ⊗8:30am-7pm Jun-Sep, 9am-5pm Oct-May) Parks Canada desk offering specialist advice on exploring the backcountry area around Lake Louise.

Lake Louise Tourism Bureau (📞403-762-8421; www.banfflakelouise.com; Samson Mall, Lake Louise village; ⊗8:30am-7pm Jun-Sep, 9am-5pm Oct-May) Information on activities and accommodations in Lake Louise village.

Parks Canada Lake Louise Visitors Centre

(📞403-522-3833; www.pc.gc.ca/en/pn-np/ab/banff; Samson Mall, Lake Louise village; ⊗8:30am-7pm Jun-Sep, 9am-5pm Oct-May) Visit Parks Canada's renovated digs for national park info and to register for backcountry hikes.

Jasper Town & Around

📞 780 / POP 4590

Arriving in Jasper Town, the first thing you may notice is how low-key it all feels. Yes, Jasper is the most important town for kilometers around, and sees nearly two million visitors each year. Yet it feels far removed from the traffic jams of Lake Louise and retains an agreeable humility that seems more reflective of its workaday railway town roots than of its modern status as a national park hub.

With only two main thoroughfares, Patricia St and Connaught Dr, holding the lion's share of businesses, you can easily explore Jasper on foot in half an hour. Sit on the lawn outside the early 20th-century log cabin at the heart of town, meditate on the murmur of the freight trains running by, and soak up the unhurried vibe. You really couldn't ask for a friendlier, more relaxing base for exploring the awe-inspiring wilderness that surrounds you.

◉ Sights

★ Jasper National Park NATIONAL PARK

(www.pc.gc.ca/jasper; day pass adult/child/family $9.80/free/19.60) Wolves, elk, caribou, beaver and bear roam freely; glaciers stretch out between stark mountain peaks; waterfalls thunder over slopes; and valleys are wide and lush, with rivers charging turbulently through them – Jasper National Park covers a diverse 11,228 sq km. Jasper is far from built up: while activities like hiking and mountain biking are well established and deservedly popular, it's still easy to experience the solitude and remoteness that abound in this park.

Some of the most popular natural wonders, like Miette Hot Springs and Maligne Canyon, are easily accessible, and many more attractions are just a short hike away. Keep a little spare time in your itinerary to take advantage of the many diversions you stumble upon – a sparkling lake to admire, a snowshoe tour to explore or a moose to watch ambling by. As the largest of Canada's Rocky Mountain parks, Jasper will quickly captivate you with its beauty and serenity.

★ Miette Hot Springs HOT SPRINGS

(www.pc.gc.ca/hotsprings; Miette Rd; adult/child/family $7.05/5.15/20.35; ⊙9am-11pm mid-Jun–Aug, 10:30am-9pm May–mid-Jun & Sep–mid-Oct) More remote than Banff's historic springs, Miette Hot Springs ('discovered' in 1909) are 61km northeast of Jasper off Hwy 16, near the park's eastern boundary. The soothing waters, kept at a pleasant 37°C (98°F) to 40°C (104°F), are surrounded by peaks and are especially enjoyable when the fall snow is drifting down and steam envelops the crowd. Raining summer evenings also make for stunning, misty conditions.

Horseshoe Lake LAKE

This idyllic, blue-green horseshoe-shaped lake just off the Icefields Pkwy is missed by many visitors, making a stopover here all the more alluring. A choice spot for a bracing summer swim or a short stroll around the perimeter, the lake is surrounded by steep cliffs and is frequented by cliff divers. It's probably safer to watch than join in.

Maligne Lake LAKE

Almost 50km from Jasper at the end of a stunning road that bears its name, 22km-long Maligne Lake is the recipient of a lot of hype. It's the largest lake in the national park and there's no denying its appeal: the baby-blue water and a craning circle of rocky, photogenic peaks are a feast for the eyes.

Jasper Skytram CABLE CAR

(📞780-852-3093; www.jaspertramway.com; Whistlers Mountain Rd; adult/child/family $50/27/125; ⊙8am-9pm late Jun-Aug, 9am-8pm mid-May–late Jun, 10am-5pm late Mar–mid-May, Sep & Oct) If the average, boring views from Jasper just aren't blowing your hair back, go for a ride on this sightseeing gondola. The seven-minute journey (departures every nine minutes) zips up through various mountain life zones to the high barren slopes of the Whistlers. From the gondola's upper station a steep 1.25km hike leads to the mountain's true summit, where views stretch for 75km. Arrive early or late to avoid midday lines. There's a small restaurant and gift shop up top.

🏃 Activities

Cycling

Jasper tops Banff for single-track mountain biking; in fact, it's one of the best places in Canada for the sport. Many rides are within striking distance of town. Flatter, on-road options include the long-distance grunt along the Icefields Parkway. The holy grail for experienced off-road cyclists is the Valley of the Five Lakes – it's varied and scenic, with plenty of places where you can let it rip. For more information, get a copy of *Mountain Biking Guide, Jasper National Park* from the Jasper Information Centre (p108).

Vicious Cycle (☑780-852-1111; www.vicious canada.com; 630 Connaught Dr, Jasper Town; bike rental per hour/day from $8/32; ⊙9am-6pm Sun-Thu, to 7pm Fri & Sat) and **The Bench Bike Shop** (☑780-852-7768; www.thebenchbikeshop.com; 606 Patricia St, Jasper Town; bike rental per hour/day from $10/30; ⊙10am-6pm) can sort out bike rentals and offer additional trail tips.

Hiking

★ Skyline Trail   HIKING
This 45.6km Rockies classic leads through awe-inspiringly rugged, wide-open high country along the crest of the Maligne Range. Most hikers allow two or three days to savor the expansive views, with overnight stops at a series of backcountry campsites or the rustic **Shovel Pass Lodge** (☑780-852-4215; www.skylinetrail.com; per person incl meals $255; ⊙late Jun-early Sep). A **shuttle** (☑780-852-3331; www.maligne adventures.com; one way adult/child $35/17.50; ⊙late Jun-late Sep) allows hikers to start at one trailhead and finish at the other.

★ Tonquin Valley Trail   HIKING
For wilderness lovers, this 53.2km out-and-back into one of Jasper's most untouched lake valleys is the experience of a lifetime. Notorious for its mosquitoes and mud, it's not for the faint-hearted, but the access route through Maccarib Pass is highly scenic, while campgrounds and a backcountry lodge offer accommodations with amazing views of Amethyst Lake and the sheer rock Ramparts.

★ Maligne Canyon   HIKING
One of Jasper's most spectacular hikes is the easy amble through this steep, narrow gorge shaped by the torrential waters of the Maligne River. The canyon at its narrowest is only a few meters wide and drops a stomach-turning 50m beneath your feet. Crossed by six bridges, it's most easily accessed from the parking area on Maligne Lake Rd.

Horseback Riding
Tonquin Valley Backcountry Lodge (p107) runs incredible, fully guided summer pack trips into the roadless Tonquin Valley, including meals and accommodations at their backcountry lodge and complimentary use of boats on Amethyst Lake. For a more leisurely horseback experience, **Jasper Riding Stables** (☑780-852-7433; www.jasper stables.com; Stables Rd, Jasper Town; 1/2/3hr rides $52/95/135; ⊙May–mid-Oct) offers enjoyable day rides lasting from one to three hours.

Skiing & Snowboarding
Jasper National Park's only downhill ski area is **Marmot Basin** (www.skimarmot.com; Marmot Basin Rd; day pass adult/child $110/89), which lies 19km southwest of town off Hwy 93A. Though not legendary, the presence of 95 runs and the longest high-speed quad chairlift in the Canadian Rockies mean Marmot is no pushover – and its relative isolation compared to the trio of ski areas in Banff means shorter lift lines.

ALISA KHLESTKOVA/SHUTTERSTOCK ©

Maligne Lake

On-site are some cross-country trails and a predictably expensive day lodge, but no overnight accommodations. Regular shuttles link to Jasper Town in season. Seriously cold weather can drift in suddenly off the mountains, so dress appropriately.

👉 Tours

Jasper Adventure Centre   OUTDOORS
(☑ 780-852-5595; www.jasperadventurecentre.com; 611 Patricia St, Jasper Town; ⊙ 8am-9pm late Jun-Aug, to 6pm May-late Jun & Sep–mid-Oct) Jasper's veteran guiding outfit runs numerous local tours, as well as some further afield to the Icefields and Lake Louise. One of their most popular trips is the three-hour Wildlife Discovery Tour (adult/child $69/35). In winter they share office space with SunDog Tour Company (☑ 780-852-4056; www.sundogtours.com; 414 Connaught Dr; ⊙ 8am-5pm), from where they organize dogsledding and ice walks in addition to their many year-round tours.

Jasper Walks & Talks   HIKING
(☑ 780-852-4994; www.walksntalks.com; 626 Connaught Dr, Jasper Town; walks per adult $65-90, per child $45-50) Longtime local resident and former Parks Canada guide Paula Beauchamp leads small groups on three- to six-hour tours with a focus on such local attractions as Maligne Canyon and Mt Edith Cavell Meadows. Bring a picnic lunch, good walking shoes, your camera and lots of questions for your very knowledgeable guide. Winter snowshoe adventures are also offered.

Maligne Lake Cruises   CRUISE
(www.banffjaspercollection.com/attractions/maligne-lake-cruise; Maligne Lake; adult/child 90min cruise $79/40, 2hr cruise $114/57; ⊙ May-Sep) These interpretive boat tours take you to the far end of Maligne Lake, to iconic Spirit Island (which, it should be noted, is not actually an island). En route, the lake shimmers in beguiling shades of blue as guides fill you in on local history and geology. Nevertheless, the price does seem rather high for the service provided.

🛏️ Sleeping

Accommodations in Jasper are generally cheaper than Banff, but that's not really saying much. The town's limited hotel and hostel rooms fill up quickly in summer, as do the cabins, bungalows and campgrounds in the surrounding countryside.

Jasper's 11 park campgrounds (four of which accept reservations) are open from mid-May to September or October, with one (Wapiti) staying open year-round. For information, visit the Parks Canada Jasper Information Centre (p108).

⭐ HI Jasper   HOSTEL $
(☑ 587-870-2395; www.hihostels.ca; 708 Sleepy Hollow Rd, Jasper Town; dm/d from $50/167; 🅿 @ 🛜) 🏊 Jasper's 157-bed HI hostel, opened two blocks from downtown in 2019 to replace the aging Whistlers Mountain facility, is a gem. The sprawling lower level houses a bevy of bright, welcoming common spaces – cozy booth seating, pool table, cafe, laundry facilities, free parking with EV charging stations, and more.

Upstairs, pairs of four-bed dorms share their own shower, toilet and sink area, while family rooms, private quads and wheelchair-accessible units are also available. There's excellent wi-fi throughout, along with individual reading lights and charging stations above each bed. A potential downside for light sleepers are the train tracks right outside the back windows – though romantics may appreciate the occasional lonesome locomotive whistle and the families of elk that sometimes bed down in the field across the street.

Jasper Downtown Hostel   HOSTEL $
(☑ 780-852-2000; www.jasperdowntownhostel.ca; 400 Patricia St, Jasper Town; dm/d from $45/140; 🛜) With Jasper's town center smack on its doorstep, this former residence has been remodeled and expanded to create simple, modern two- to 10-bed dorms, many with en suite bathrooms, along with comfortable private rooms sleeping one to three. Upstairs rooms are brighter, with wooden floors, while common areas include a well-equipped kitchen, a spacious front patio and a simple lounge.

Athabasca Hotel   HOTEL $$
(☑ 780-852-3386; www.athabascahotel.com; 510 Patricia St, Jasper Town; r without/with bath $139/239, 1-/2-bedroom ste $395/425; 🅿 @ 🛜) Around since 1929, the Atha-B (as it's known) is the best budget hotel in town. A taxidermist's dream, with animal heads crowding the lobby, it has small, clean rooms with wooden and brass furnishings and thick, wine-colored carpets. Less expensive rooms share a bathroom. Dated but not worn, it feels like you're staying at Grandma's (if Grandma liked to hunt).

Becker's Chalets

CHALET $$

(📞 780-852-3779; www.beckerschalets.com; Hwy 93; d/q chalet from $200/225; 🅿🤖) Just 6km south of Jasper Town and paces from the northern entrance to the Icefields Pkwy, this complex of 118 chalets has something for everyone – from 33 cute 1930s-vintage 'heritage' cabins to a block of big modern four-plexes popular with families and European tour groups. Rates here are among Jasper's cheapest, even if it's a bit of a mob scene.

★Patricia Lake Bungalows

BUNGALOW $$$

(📞 780-852-3560; www.patricialakebungalows. com; Patricia Lake Rd; bungalows $199-510) Reminiscent of an earlier era, this charming assemblage of bungalows sits placidly at the end of a dead-end road on the shores of lovely Patricia Lake, 5km north of Jasper Town. Owned by the same family for nearly half a century, it's the kind of place where you can truly leave the modern world (and the summer crowds) behind.

★Tonquin Valley Backcountry Lodge

LODGE $$$

(📞 780-852-3909; www.tonquinvalley.com; per person incl meals summer/winter $325/185; ⊙ mid-Feb–Mar & Jul–mid-Sep) These rustic cabins are located on Amethyst Lake, deep in Jasper's backcountry. Linen, a wood-burning stove, home-cooked meals and stunning views keep you cozy and you get use of a boat or canoe. There's a minimum two-night stay for hikers and skiers, or you can join a multiday horseback-riding trek to reach the lodge (five days from $2500).

✕ Eating

Jasper's cuisine is mainly hearty post-hiking fare. Most of the restaurants are located in town around Connaught Dr and Patricia St. Outlying areas such as Maligne Lake and the Whistlers have cafeteria-style restaurants that close in the winter.

★Other Paw Bakery

CAFE $

(📞 780-852-2253; www.bearspawbakery.com; 610 Connaught Dr, Jasper Town; mains $5-13; ⊙ 7am-6pm) An offshoot of the original Bear's Paw bakery around the corner, the Other Paw offers the same addictive mix of breads, pastries, muffins and coffee – while also serving up tasty sandwiches, salads, soups and well-stuffed wraps.

LOOK TO THE SKIES

For ten days in late October, **Dark Sky Festival** (www.jasperdarksky.travel; ⊙ late Oct) holds events celebrating space and the night sky. Hear talks by astronauts, astronomers and astrophotographers, listen to the symphony under the stars, see the aurora borealis reflected in a glacial lake and gaze through a telescope into the great beyond. There are some free events, but the big hitters sell out months in advance.

Patricia Street Deli

SANDWICHES $

(📞 780-852-4814; www.facebook.com/patricia streetdeli; 610 Patricia St, Jasper Town; sandwiches $9.50-12; ⊙ 10am-7pm) Come to the Patricia Street Deli hungry – really hungry. Homemade bread is made into generously filled sandwiches by people who are just as generous with their smiles and hiking tips. Choose from a huge list of fillings, including various pestos, chutneys, veggies and meat cuts. Join the queue and satiate your ravenous backcountry appetite.

Coco's Cafe

CAFE $

(📞 780-852-4550; www.cocoscafe.ca; 608b Patricia St, Jasper Town; mains $9-15; ⊙ 8am-4pm; 🖉) 🖋 If you're looking for breakfast, you can't go wrong at Coco's. There's not much room inside, but many are happy to cram in to plan hikes and trade bear sightings. There's plenty of locally sourced, vegan, veggie and celiac-friendly fare on the menu, while carnivores are kept happy with Montreal smoked meat, pulled pork and lox.

For lunch, try the grown-up grilled cheese sandwich with apple and onion chutney.

Olive Bistro

MEDITERRANEAN $$

(📞 780-852-5222; www.olivebistro.ca; Pyramid Lake Rd, Jasper Town; mains $14-35; ⊙ 4-10pm May-Oct, 5-9pm Nov-Apr; 🖉) This casual restaurant with big booths has a classy menu. Main dishes such as slow-braised organic lamb shank, elk rigatoni or a vegan 'dragon bowl' come sandwiched between appetizers of white truffle scallops and indulgent desserts like a gourmet banana split. In summer, enjoy excellent cocktails during the 4pm to 6pm happy hour; in winter, there's live music twice monthly.

★ Maligne Canyon
Wilderness Kitchen
BARBECUE $$$

(✆844-762-6713; www.banffjaspercollection.com; Maligne Canyon Rd; lunch mains $16-26, dinner $55; ⊙8am-10pm May-Sep, 9am-4pm Sun-Fri, to 10pm Sat Oct-Apr) The outdoor deck at the edge of gorgeous Maligne Canyon is temptation enough to dine here. But the real clincher is the cornucopia of local meats, shown off to full advantage in the house special Maligne Canyon Platter: grilled venison sausage, smoked chicken, glazed baby back pork ribs, and barbecue Alberta beef brisket slow-cooked for 16 hours.

★ Raven Bistro
MEDITERRANEAN $$$

(✆780-852-5151; www.theravenbistro.com; 504 Patricia St, Jasper Town; lunch mains $16-27, dinner mains $28-46; ⊙11:30am-11pm; 🞉) This cozy, tastefully designed bistro offers vegetarian dishes, encourages shared plates and earns a loyal clientele with sublime offerings like Kaffir lime–coconut seafood pot or lamb shank glazed with fresh mint, horseradish, honey and Dijon mustard. Not in a lunch-dinner mood? Try the 'late riser' breakfast skillet, or come for happy hour (3pm to 5:30pm daily).

🍷 Drinking & Nightlife

There are a surprising number of liquor stores in town, along with a great local microbrewery. Many hotels have a bar and there are are a couple of pubs where you can kick back with a brew. The clubbing scene is questionable.

★ SnowDome Coffee Bar
COFFEE

(✆780-852-3852; http://snowdome.coffee; 607 Patricia St, Jasper Town; ⊙7am-8pm; 🞉) Some of Jasper's best damn coffee is – no joke! – served at this former Coin Clean Laundry, now reincarnated as a cafe-gallery-community hangout. Beyond the stellar espresso, SnowDome bakes killer muffins (still oven-warm at opening time) and promotes good karma with its free mug basket and 'pay it forward' bulletin board where you can prepurchase coffee for an unsuspecting future customer.

Folding Mountain Taproom
MICROBREWERY

(✆780-817-6287; www.foldingmountain.com; 49321 Hwy 16, Jasper East; ⊙11am-10pm) This up-and-coming microbrewery draws a boisterous mix of locals from nearby Hinton and travelers heading to or from the wilderness. Test the waters with a four-beer sampler (choose from Flash Flood IPA, Alpine Cranberry Sour or a dozen other brews on tap), then stick around for excellent burgers, salads and other pub grub. It's just 5km outside Jasper's eastern park gate.

Jasper Brewing Co
BREWERY

(✆780-852-4111; www.jasperbrewingco.ca; 624 Connaught Dr, Jasper Town; ⊙11:30am-1am) 🖉 This brewpub was the first of its kind in a Canadian national park, using glacial water to make its fine ales, including the signature Rockhopper IPA and Jasper the Bear honey beer. It's a perennial favorite hangout for locals and tourists alike, with TVs and a good food menu.

Downstream Lounge
BAR

(✆780-852-9449; www.facebook.com/DSjasper; 620 Connaught Dr, Jasper Town; ⊙5pm-2am) This is likely the best-stocked bar in town, with a wide array of whiskeys, vodkas and other alcoholic indulgences – and a bar staff who know how to use them. There's some awesome food to keep your head above water and, often, live music.

ℹ️ Information

Parks Canada Jasper Information Centre
(✆780-852-6176; www.pc.gc.ca/jasper; 500 Connaught Dr, Jasper Town; ⊙9am-7pm mid-May–early Oct, to 5pm rest of year) Parks Canada operates a well-staffed and helpful info desk in this wonderful midtown building – Jasper's oldest, dating from 1913. Directly adjacent are the local tourist information stand, plus an excellent gift shop.

Tourism Jasper (✆780-852-6236; www.jasper.travel; 500 Connaught Dr, Jasper Town; ⊙9am-7pm mid-May–early Oct, to 5pm rest of year) Jasper's municipal tourist office, directly adjacent to the Parks Canada info center at the heart of town, offers a wealth of information about area activities and accommodations.

ROAD TRIP ESSENTIALS

Canada Driving Guide

Canada is a fabulous place for road trips, with an extensive network of highways, breathtaking scenery and friendly locals to help out if you should lose your way.

DRIVER'S LICENSE & DOCUMENTS

In most provinces, visitors can legally drive for up to three months with their home driver's license. In some, such as British Columbia, this is extended to six months.

If you're spending considerable time in Canada, think about getting an International Driving Permit (IDP), which is valid for one year. Your automobile association at home can issue one for a small fee. Always carry your home license together with the IDP.

Driving Fast Facts

➡ **Right or left?** Drive on the right
➡ **Legal driving age** 16
➡ **Top speed limit** Varies by province; 90km/h in Prince Edward Island, 100km/h in Ontario and 120km/h in British Columbia
➡ **Best radio station** The commercial-free Canadian Broadcasting Corporation (CBC)

INSURANCE

Canadian law requires liability insurance for all vehicles, to cover you for damage caused to property and people.

➡ The minimum requirement is $200,000 in all provinces except Québec, where it is $50,000.

➡ Americans traveling to Canada in their own car should ask their insurance company for a Nonresident Interprovince Motor Vehicle Liability Insurance Card (commonly known as a 'yellow card'), which is accepted as evidence of financial responsibility anywhere in Canada. Although not mandatory, it may come in handy in an accident.

➡ Car-rental agencies offer liability insurance. Collision Damage Waivers (CDW) reduce or eliminate the amount you'll have to reimburse the rental company if there's damage to the car itself. Some credit cards cover CDW for a certain rental period if you use the card to pay for the rental and decline the policy offered by the rental company. Always check with your card issuer to see what coverage it offers in Canada.

➡ Personal accident insurance (PAI) covers you and any passengers for medical costs incurred as a result of an accident. If your travel insurance or your health-insurance policy at home does this as well (and most do, but check), then this is one expense you can do without.

RENTAL
Car

To rent a car in Canada you generally need to be at least 25 years old (some companies will rent to drivers between the ages of 21 and 24 for an additional charge); hold a valid driver's license (an international one may be required if you're not from an English- or French-speaking country); and have a major credit card.

Renta-car rates generally include unlimited mileage, but expect surcharges for additional drivers and one-way rentals. Major international car-rental companies usually have branches at airports, train stations and in city centers. In Canada, on-the-spot rentals often are more expensive than pre-booked packages (ie cars booked with a flight or in advance).

Child and infant safety seats are legally required; reserve them (around $15 per day, or $50 per trip) when booking your car.

International car-rental companies with hundreds of branches nationwide include:

Avis (☑800-230-4898; www.avis.com)

Budget (☑800-268-8900, French 800-268-8970; www.budget.com)

Dollar (☑800-800-5252; www.dollar canada.ca)

Enterprise (☑844-307-8008; www.enterprise.ca)

Hertz (☑800-654-3131; www.hertz.com)

National (☑toll free 844-307-8014; www.nationalcar.ca)

Practicar (☑toll free 800-327-0116; www.practicar.ca) Often has lower rates. It's also affiliated with Backpackers Hostels Canada and Hostelling International.

Thrifty (☑800-334-1705; www.thrifty canada.ca)

Motorcycle

Several companies offer motorcycle rentals and tours. A Harley Heritage Softail Classic costs about $210 per day, including liability insurance and 200km mileage. Some companies have minimum rental

Canada Playlist

Feist Mushaboom

Wheat Kings The Tragically Hip

Keep the Car Running Arcade Fire

Prémonition Coeur de Pirate

Electric Pow Wow Drum The Halluci Nation

Bridge to Nowhere Sam Roberts

Tôt ou Tard Eli Rose

I Don't Know The Sheepdogs

Colossus of Rhodes The New Pornographers

Crabbuckit K-OS

Fous n'Importe Où Charlotte Cardin & CRi

Heart of Gold Neil Young

When the Night Feels My Song Bedouin Soundclash

Driving Tips

➡ Never let the gas tank go below a third of a tank, even if you think there's cheaper fuel up the road. When traveling out west, always fill up before heading to your next destination. Sometimes, the next station is a long way off!

➡ In some areas you can drive for hours without cell service, so plan carefully for emergencies.

➡ Moose, deer and elk are common on rural roadways, especially at night. There's no contest between a 534kg bull moose and a Subaru, so keep your eyes peeled.

➡ A word for Canada's southern neighbors: don't forget that speed limits are in kilometers - not miles - per hour!

Road Trip Websites

Canadian Automobile Association (www.caa.ca)
Offers services, including 24-hour emergency roadside assistance, to members of international affiliates, such as AAA in the USA, AA in the UK and ADAC in Germany. The club also offers trip-planning advice, free maps, travel-agency services and a range of discounts on hotels, car rentals etc. Autoclub membership is a handy thing to have in Canada.

Canada Road Conditions (https://www.th.gov.bc.ca/drivebc_supp/canada_map.htm) Check the status of road conditions in all 13 provinces and territories.

---

periods, which can be as much as seven days. Riding a hog is especially popular in British Columbia.

Cycle BC (☑604-709-5663; http://cyclebc.ca) Tours and rentals out of Victoria and Vancouver in British Columbia.

McScoots Motorcycle & Scooter Rentals (☑250-763-4668; www.mcscoots.com) Big selection of Harleys; also operates motorcycle tours. It's based in Kelowna, British Columbia.

RVs & Campervans

The RV market is biggest in the west, with specialized agencies in Calgary, Edmonton, Whitehorse and Vancouver. For summer travel, book as early as possible. The base cost is roughly $250 per day in high season for smaller vehicles, although insurance, fees and taxes add a hefty chunk to that. Diesel-fueled RVs have considerably lower running costs.

Canadream Campers (☑925-255-8383; www.canadream.com) Based in Calgary, with rentals (including one-way rentals) in eight cities, including Vancouver, Whitehorse, Toronto and Halifax.

Cruise Canada (☑403-291-4963; www.cruisecanada.com) Offers three sizes of RVs. Locations in Halifax, and in central and western Canada; offers one-way rentals.

BRINGING YOUR OWN VEHICLE

There's minimal hassle driving into Canada from the USA, as long as you have your vehicle's registration papers, proof of liability insurance and your home driver's license.

MAPS & APPS

➡ **National Geographic Road Atlas** is one of the best ink-and-paper maps, with special attention paid to national parks and forests.

➡ **Google Maps** (http://maps.google.com) Turn-by-turn driving directions with estimated traffic delays. Be sure to download offline maps so you have mapping details when you lack cell-phone service.

➡ **Waze** (www.waze.com) Popular, free crowd-sourced traffic and navigation app.

➡ **GasBuddy** (www.gasbuddy.com) Website and app that finds the cheapest places to gas up nearby.

➡ Most tourist offices distribute free provincial road maps.

➡ You can also download and print maps from GeoBase (http://geogratis.gc.ca).

ROAD CONDITIONS

Road conditions are generally good, but there are a few things to keep in mind.

Fierce winters can leave potholes the size of landmine craters. Be prepared to swerve. Winter travel in general can be hazardous due to heavy snow and ice, which may cause roads and bridges to close periodically. **Transport Canada** (☑613-990-2309; www.tc.gc.ca/en/transport-canada.html) provides links to road conditions and construction zones for each province.

If you're driving in winter or in remote areas, make sure your vehicle is equipped with four-season radial or snow tires, and emergency supplies in case you're stranded.

ROAD RULES

➡ Canadians drive on the right-hand side of the road.

➡ Seat belt use is compulsory. Children who weigh less than 18kg must be strapped into child-booster seats, except infants, who must be in a rear-facing safety seat.

➡ Motorcyclists must wear helmets and drive with their headlights on.

➡ Distances and speed limits are posted in kilometers. The speed limit is generally 40km/h to 50km/h in cities and 90km/h to 110km/h outside town.

➡ Slow down to 60km/h when passing emergency vehicles (such as police cars and ambulances) stopped on the roadside with their lights flashing.

➡ Turning right at red lights after coming to a full stop is permitted in all provinces (except where road signs prohibit it, and on the island of Montréal, where it's always a no-no). There's a national propensity for running red lights, however, so don't assume 'right of way' at intersections.

➡ Driving while using a hand-held cell phone is illegal in Canada. Fines are hefty.

➡ Radar detectors are not allowed in most of Canada (Alberta, British Columbia and Saskatchewan are the exceptions). If you're caught driving with a radar detector, even one that isn't being operated, you could receive a fine of $1000 and your device may be confiscated.

➡ The blood-alcohol limit for drivers is 0.08%, but provincial limits can be lower. Driving while drunk or high is a criminal offense.

PARKING

Free parking is plentiful in small towns and rural areas, but scarce and often expensive in cities. Municipal parking meters and centralized pay stations usually accept coins and credit or debit cards.

Road Distances (km)

	Banff	Calgary	Edmonton	Halifax	Inuvik	Jasper	Montréal	Ottawa	Québec City	St John's	Toronto	Vancouver	Whitehorse	Winnipeg
Calgary	130													
Edmonton	410	290												
Halifax	4900	4810	4850											
Inuvik	3440	3515	3220	8110										
Jasper	280	415	370	5250	3150									
Montréal	3700	3550	3605	1240	6820	3950								
Ottawa	3450	3340	3410	1440	6620	3770	200							
Québec City	3900	3800	3880	1020	7060	4210	250							
St John's	6200	6100	6150	1480	9350	6480	2530	2730	2310					
Toronto	3400	3400	3470	1790	6680	3820	550	450	800	3090				
Vancouver	850	970	1160	5880	3630	790	4580	4350	4830	7130	4360			
Whitehorse	2210	2290	2010	6830	1220	1930	5620	5390	5840	8150	5450	2400		
Winnipeg	1450	1325	1330	3520	4550	1670	2280	2140	2520	4820	2220	2290	3340	
Yellowknife	1800	1790	1510	6340	3770	1590	5050	4900	5350	7620	4950	2370	2540	2800

These distances are approximate only.

Driving Problem-Buster

What should I do if my car breaks down? Put on your hazard lights (flashers) and carefully pull over to the side of the road. Call the roadside emergency assistance number of your car-rental company or, if you're driving your own car, your automobile association.

What if I have an accident? If it's safe to do so, pull over to the side of the road. For minor collisions with no major property damage or bodily injuries, be sure to exchange driver's license and auto-insurance information with the other driver, then file a report with your insurance provider or notify your car-rental company as soon as possible. If you distrust the other party, call the police, who will fill out an objective report. For major accidents, call ⬛911 and wait for the police and emergency services to arrive.

What should I do if I am stopped by the police? Be courteous. Don't get out of the car unless asked. Keep your hands where the officer can see them (eg on the steering wheel). For traffic violations, there is usually a 30-day period to pay a fine; most matters can be handled by mail. Police can legally give roadside sobriety checks to assess if you've been drinking or using drugs.

What should I do if my car gets towed? Immediately call the local police in the town or city that you're in and ask where to pick up your car. Towing and hourly or daily storage fees can quickly total hundreds of dollars.

What if I can't find anywhere to stay? If you're stuck and it's getting late, it's best not to keep driving on aimlessly – just pull into the next roadside chain motel or hotel with the 'Vacancy' light lit up.

When parking on the street, carefully read all posted regulations and restrictions (eg 30-minute maximum, no parking during scheduled street-cleaning hours) and pay attention to colored curbs, or you may be ticketed and towed. In some towns and cities, overnight street parking is prohibited downtown and in designated areas reserved for local residents with permits.

At city parking garages and lots, expect to pay at least $2 per hour and $12 to $40 for all-day or overnight parking.

FUEL

Most gas stations in Canada are self-service. You'll find them on highways outside of most towns, though the options are few and far between in sparsely populated areas.

Gas is sold in liters (3.78L equals one US gallon). The current cost for regular fuel in Canada ranges from $1.10 to $1.55. Prices are higher in remote areas, with Yellowknife usually setting the national record; drivers in Calgary typically pay the least for gas.

Fuel prices are usually lower in the USA, so fill up south of the border if that's an option.

SAFETY

Vehicle theft, break-ins and vandalism are a problem mostly in urban areas. Be sure to lock your vehicle's doors, leave the windows rolled up and use any anti-theft devices that have been installed (eg car alarm, steering-wheel lock). Do not leave any valuables visible inside your vehicle; instead, stow them in the trunk before arriving at your destination, or else take them with you once you've parked.

Canada Travel Guide

GETTING THERE & AWAY

AIR

Airports & Airlines

Toronto is far and away Canada's busiest airport, followed by Vancouver. The international gateways you're most likely to use:

Calgary (Calgary International Airport; www.yyc.com)

Edmonton (Edmonton International Airport; http://flyeia.com)

Halifax (Halifax Stanfield International Airport; http://halifaxstanfield.ca)

Montréal (Montréal Trudeau International Airport; www.admtl.com)

Ottawa (Ottawa International Airport; http://yow.ca)

St John's (St John's International Airport; http://stjohnsairport.com)

Toronto (Toronto Pearson International Airport; www.torontopearson.com)

Vancouver (Vancouver International Airport; www.yvr.ca)

Winnipeg (Winnipeg International Airport; www.waa.ca)

Air Canada (www.aircanada.com), the national flagship carrier, is considered one of the world's safest airlines. All major global airlines fly to Canada. Other companies based in the country and serving international destinations:

WestJet (www.westjet.com) Calgary-based low-cost carrier serving destinations throughout Canada as well as across the US and Caribbean.

Porter Airlines (www.flyporter.com) Flies around eastern Canada and to US cities, including Boston, Chicago, Washington, DC, and New York.

Air Transat (www.airtransat.com) Charter airline from major Canadian cities to holiday destinations (ie southern USA and Caribbean in winter, Europe in summer).

CAR & MOTORCYCLE

The highway system of the continental USA connects directly with the Canadian highway system at numerous points along the border. These Canadian highways then meet up with the east–west Trans-Canada Hwy further north. Between the Yukon Territory and Alaska, the main routes are the Alaska, Klondike and Haines Hwys.

If you're driving into Canada, you'll need the vehicle's registration papers, proof of liability insurance and your home driver's license. Cars rented in the USA can usually be driven into Canada and back, but make sure your rental agreement says so. If you're driving a car registered in someone else's name, bring a letter from the owner authorizing use of the vehicle in Canada.

SEA

Ferry

Various ferry services on the coasts connect the USA and Canada:

➡ Bar Harbor, Maine, to Yarmouth, NS: **Bay Ferries Limited** (www.ferries.ca/thecat)

➡ Eastport, Maine, to Deer Island, NB: **East Coast Ferries** (www.eastcoastferriesltd.com)

➡ Seattle, WA, to Victoria, BC: **Victoria Clipper** (www.clippervacations.com)

➡ Ketchikan, Alaska, to Prince Rupert, BC: **Alaska Marine Highway System** (www.ferryalaska.com)

➡ Bella Bella, BC, to Prince Rupert, BC: **BC Ferries** (www.bcferries.com)

➡ Sandusky, Ohio, to Pelee Island, ON: **Pelee Island Transportation Service** (www.ontarioferries.com)

➡ Port Angeles, WA, to Victoria, BC; **Black Ball Ferry** (www.cohoferry.com)

➡ Anacortes, WA, to Sidney, BC; **Washington State Ferries** (www.wsdot.wa.gov/ferries)

Freighters

An adventurous, though not necessarily inexpensive, way to travel to or from Canada is aboard a cargo ship. Freighters carry between three and 12 passengers and, though considerably less luxurious than cruise ships, they give a salty taste of life at sea. **Maris Freighter Cruises** (www.freightercruises.com) has more information on the ever-changing routes.

TRAIN

Amtrak (www.amtrak.com) and **VIA Rail Canada** (www.viarail.ca) run three routes between the USA and Canada: two in the east and one in the west. Customs inspections happen at the border, not upon boarding.

Train Routes & Fares

Route	Duration (hr)	Frequency (daily)	Fare (US$)
New York–Toronto (Maple Leaf)	13¾	1	131
New York–Montréal (Adirondack)	12	1	70
Seattle–Vancouver (Cascades)	4	2	41

DIRECTORY A–Z

ACCESSIBLE TRAVEL

Canada is making progress when it comes to easing the everyday challenges facing people with disabilities, especially those who have mobility requirements.

➡ Many public buildings, including museums, tourist offices, train stations, shopping malls and cinemas, have access ramps and/or lifts. Most public restrooms feature extra-wide stalls equipped with hand rails. Many pedestrian crossings have sloping curbs.

➡ Newer and recently remodeled hotels, especially chain hotels, have rooms with extra-wide doors and spacious bathrooms.

➡ Interpretive centers at national and provincial parks are usually accessible, and many parks have trails that can be navigated in wheelchairs.

➡ Car-rental agencies offer hand-controlled vehicles and vans with wheelchair lifts at no additional charge, but you must reserve them well in advance.

➡ Download Lonely Planet's free Accessible Travel guides from http://lptravel.to/AccessibleTravel.

➡ For accessible air, bus, rail and ferry transportation, check **Access to Travel** (www.accesstotravel.gc.ca), the federal government's website. In general, most transportation agencies can accommodate people with disabilities if you make your needs known when booking.

Other organizations specializing in the needs of travelers with disabilities:

Mobility International (www.miusa.org) Advises travelers with disabilities on mobility issues and runs an educational exchange · program.

Society for Accessible Travel & Hospitality (www.sath.org) Travelers with disabilities share tips and blogs.

ACCOMMODATIONS

In popular destinations, such as Ottawa, Banff and Jasper, it pays to book ahead in the height of the summer, especially during major festivals, and in the ski season.

B&Bs From purpose-built villas to heritage homes or someone's spare room, they are often the most atmospheric lodgings.

Camping Campgrounds are plentiful; private grounds often have fancier facilities.

Hostels Young backpacker hangouts, but favored by outdoor adventurers in remoter regions.

Hotels From standard to luxurious with a burgeoning number of boutique options.

Motels Dotting the highways into town, these are often family-run affairs that offer the most bang for your buck.

Seasons

➤ Peak season is summer, basically June through August, when prices are highest.

➤ It's best to book ahead during summer, as well as during ski season at winter resorts, and during holidays and major events, as rooms can be scarce.

➤ Some properties close down altogether in the off-season.

B&Bs

➤ **Bed & Breakfast Online** (http://m. bbcanada.com) is the main booking agency for properties nationwide.

➤ In Canada, B&Bs (*gîtes* in French) are essentially converted or purpose-built private homes whose owners live on-site. People who like privacy may find B&Bs too intimate, as walls are rarely soundproof and it's usual to mingle with your hosts and other guests.

➤ Standards vary widely, sometimes even within a single B&B. The cheapest rooms tend to be small, with few amenities and a shared bathroom. Nicer ones have added features

such as a balcony, a fireplace and an en-suite bathroom.

➤ Breakfast is always included in the rates (though it might be continental instead of a full cooked affair).

➤ Not all B&Bs accept children.

➤ Minimum stays (usually two nights) are common, and many B&Bs are only open seasonally.

Camping

➤ Canada is filled with campgrounds – some federal or provincial, others privately owned.

➤ The official season runs from May to September, but exact dates vary by location.

➤ Facilities vary widely. Backcountry sites offer little more than pit toilets and fire rings, and have no potable water. Unserviced (tent) campgrounds come with access to drinking water and a washroom with toilets and sometimes showers. The best-equipped sites feature flush toilets and hot showers, and water, electrical and sewer hookups for recreational vehicles (RVs).

➤ Private campgrounds sometimes cater only to trailers (caravans) and RVs, and may feature convenience stores, playgrounds and swimming pools. It is a good idea to phone ahead to make sure the size of sites and the services provided at a particular campground are suitable for your vehicle.

➤ Most government-run sites are available on a first-come, first-served basis and fill up quickly, especially in July and August. Several national parks participate in Parks Canada's **camping reservation program** (☎519-826-5391; http://reservation.pc.gc.ca; reservation fee online/call center $11/13.50), which is a convenient way to make sure you get a spot.

➤ Nightly camping fees in national and provincial parks range from $25 to $35 (a bit more for full-hookup sites); fire permits often cost a few dollars extra. Backcountry camping costs about $10 per night. Private campgrounds tend to be a bit pricier. British Columbia's parks, in particular, have seen a hefty rate increase in recent years.

➡ Some campgrounds remain open for maintenance year-round and may let you camp at a reduced rate in the off-season. This can be great in late autumn or early spring, when there's hardly a soul about. Winter camping, though, is only for the hardy.

Hotels & Motels

Most hotels are part of international chains, and the newer ones are designed for either the luxury market or businesspeople, with in-room cable TV and wi-fi. Many also have swimming pools and fitness and business centers. Rooms with two double or queen-sized beds sleep up to four people, although there is usually a small surcharge for the third and fourth people. Many places advertise 'kids stay free,' but sometimes you have to pay extra for a crib or a rollaway (portable bed).

In Canada, like the USA (both lands of the automobile), motels are ubiquitous. They dot the highways and cluster in groups on the outskirts of towns and cities. Although most motel rooms won't win any style awards, they're usually clean and comfortable and offer good value for travelers. Many regional motels remain typical mom-and-pop operations, but plenty of North American chains have also opened up across the country.

DISCOUNT CARDS

Discounts are commonly offered for seniors, children, families and people with disabilities, though no special cards are issued (you get the savings on-site when you pay). AAA and other automobile association members can also receive various travel-related discounts.

International Student Identity Card (www.isic.org) Provides students with discounts on travel insurance and admission to museums and other sights. There are also cards for those who are under 26 years but not students, and for full-time teachers.

Parks Canada Discovery Pass (adult/family $68/137; www.pc.gc.ca) Provides access to more than 100 national parks and historic sites for a year. Can pay for itself in as few as seven visits; also provides quicker entry into sites. Note that there's no charge for kids under 18 years, and a 'family' can include up to seven people in a vehicle, even if they're unrelated.

Many cities have discount cards for local attractions, such as the following:

Montréal Museum Pass (www.musees montreal.org; $75)

Ottawa Museums Passport (www.museumspassport.ca; $35)

Toronto CityPASS (www.citypass.com/toronto; adult/child $73/50)

Vanier Park ExplorePass (Vancouver; www.spacecentre.ca/explore-pass; adult/child $42.50/36.50)

Practicalities

Newspapers The most widely available newspaper is the Toronto-based *Globe and Mail*. Other principal dailies are the *Montréal Gazette*, *Ottawa Citizen*, *Toronto Star* and *Vancouver Sun*. *Maclean's* is Canada's weekly news magazine.

Radio & TV The Canadian Broadcasting Corporation (CBC) is the dominant nationwide network for both radio and TV. The CTV Television Network is its major competition.

Smoking Banned in all restaurants, bars and other public venues nationwide. This includes tobacco, vaping and cannabis.

Weights & Measures Canada officially uses the metric system, but imperial measurements are used for many day-to-day purposes.

ELECTRICITY

Type A
120V/60Hz

Type B
120V/60Hz

FOOD

Canadian cuisine is nothing if not eclectic, a casserole of food cultures blended together from centuries of immigration. Poutine (French fries topped with gravy and cheese curds), Montréal-style bagels, salmon jerky and pierogi jostle for comfort-food attention. For something more refined,

Eating Price Ranges

The following price ranges are for main dishes:

$ less than $15

$$ $15–25

$$$ more than $25

Montréal, Toronto and Vancouver have well-seasoned fine-dining scenes, while regions across the country have rediscovered the unique ingredients grown, foraged and produced on their doorsteps – bringing distinctive seafood, artisan cheeses and lip-smacking produce to menus.

It's worth booking ahead for popular places, especially on the weekend – which, in the Canadian restaurant world, includes Thursdays. Most cafes and budget restaurants don't accept reservations.

Local Flavors

Starting from the east, the main dish of the Maritime provinces is lobster – boiled in the pot and served with a little butter – and the best place to sample it is a community hall 'kitchen party' on Prince Edward Island. Dip into some chunky potato salad and hearty seafood chowder while waiting for your crustacean to arrive, but don't eat too much; you'll need room for the mountainous fruit pie coming your way afterward.

Next door, Nova Scotia visitors should save their appetites for butter-soft Digby scallops and rustic Lunenburg sausage, while the favored meals of nearby Newfoundland and Labrador often combine rib-sticking dishes of cod cheeks and sweet snow crab. If you're feeling really ravenous, gnaw on a slice of seal-flipper pie – a dish you're unlikely to forget in a hurry.

Québec is the world's largest maple-syrup producer, processing an annual 60 million liters (13.2 million gallons) of the syrup used on pancakes and as an ingredient in myriad other dishes. In this French-influenced province, fine food is a lifeblood for the locals, who happily sit down to lengthy dinners where the accompanying wine and conversation flow in equal measures.

The province's cosmopolitan Montréal has long claimed to be the nation's fine-dining capital, but there's an appreciation of food here at all levels that also includes hearty pea soups, exquisite cheeses and tasty pâtés sold at bustling markets. In addition, there's also that national dish, poutine, waiting to clog your arteries, plus smoked-meat deli sandwiches.

Ontario – especially Toronto – is a microcosm of Canada's melting pot of cuisines. Like Québec, maple syrup is a super-sweet flavoring of choice here, and it's found in decadent desserts such as beavertails (fried, sugared dough) and on breakfast pancakes the size of Frisbees. Head south to the Niagara Peninsula wine region and you'll also discover restaurants fusing contemporary approaches and traditional local ingredients, such as fish from the Great Lakes.

Nunavut in the Arctic Circle is Canada's newest territory, but it has a long history of Inuit food, offering a real culinary adventure. Served in some restaurants (but more often in family homes – make friends with locals and they may invite you in for a feast), regional specialties include boiled seal, raw frozen char. You may also encounter *maktaaq* – whale skin cut into small pieces and swallowed whole.

In contrast, the central provinces of Manitoba, Saskatchewan and Alberta have their own deep-seated culinary ways. The latter, Canada's cowboy country, is the nation's beef capital – you'll find top-notch Alberta steak on menus at leading restaurants across the country. If you're offered 'prairie oysters' here, though, you might want to know (or maybe you'd prefer not to!) that they're bull's testicles, prepared in a variety of ways designed to take your mind off their origin. In the Rockies things get wilder – try elk, bison and even moose.

There's an old Eastern European influence over the border in Manitoba, where immigrant Ukrainians have added comfort food staples such as pierogi and thick, spicy sausages. Head next door to prairie-land Saskatchewan for dessert. The province's heaping fruit pies are its most striking culinary contribution, especially when prepared with tart Saskatoon berries.

In the far west, British Columbians have traditionally fed themselves from the sea and the fertile farmlands of the interior. Okanagan Valley peaches, cherries and blueberries – best purchased from seasonal roadside stands throughout the region – are the staple of many summer diets. But it's the seafood that attracts the lion's share of culinary fans. Tuck into succulent wild salmon, juicy Fanny Bay oysters and velvet-soft scallops and you may decide you've stumbled on foodie nirvana. There's also a large and ever-growing influence of Asian food in BC's Lower Mainland.

INTERNET ACCESS

➡ It's easy to find internet access. Libraries and community agencies in practically every town provide free wi-fi and computers for public use. The only downsides are that usage time is limited (usually 30 minutes), and some facilities have erratic hours.

➡ Internet cafes are scarce, limited to the main tourist areas in only certain towns; access generally starts around $2 per hour.

➡ Wi-fi is widely available. Most lodgings have it (in-room, with good speed), as do many restaurants, bars and Tim Hortons coffee shops.

LGBTIQ+ TRAVELERS

Canada is tolerant when it comes to LGBTIQ+ people, though this outlook is more common in the big cities than in rural areas. Same-sex marriage is legal throughout the country (Canada was the fourth country in the world to legalize same-sex marriage, in 2005).

Montréal, Toronto and Vancouver are by far Canada's gayest cities, each with a humming nightlife scene, publications and lots of associations and support groups. All have sizable Pride celebrations, too, which attract big crowds.

Attitudes remain more conservative in the northern regions. Throughout Nunavut, and to a lesser extent the Northwest Territories, there are some retrogressive attitudes toward homosexuality. The Yukon, in contrast, is more like British Columbia, with a live-and-let-live West Coast attitude.

The following are good resources for LGBTIQ+ travel; they include Canadian information, though not all are exclusive to the region:

Damron (www.damron.com) Publishes several travel guides; gay-friendly tour operators are listed on the website, too.

Out Traveler (www.outtraveler.com) Gay travel magazine.

Purple Roofs (www.purpleroofs.com) Website listing queer accommodations, travel agencies and tours worldwide.

Queer Events (www.queerevents.ca) A general resource for finding events that are aimed at the gay community.

Xtra (www.xtra.ca) Source for gay and lesbian news nationwide.

MONEY

➜ All prices quoted are in Canadian dollars ($), unless stated otherwise.

➜ Canadian coins come in 5¢ (nickel), 10¢ (dime), 25¢ (quarter), $1 (loonie) and $2 (toonie or twoonie) denominations. The gold-colored loonie features the loon, a common Canadian waterbird, while the two-toned toonie is decorated with a polar bear. Canada phased out its 1¢ (penny) coin in 2012.

➜ Paper currency comes in $5 (blue), $10 (purple), $20 (green) and $50 (red) denominations. The $100 (brown) and larger bills are less common. The newest bills in circulation – which have enhanced security features – are actually a polymer-based material; they feel more like plastic than paper.

➜ For changing money in the larger cities, currency exchange offices may offer better conditions than banks.

ATMs

➜ Many grocery and convenience stores, airports and bus, train and ferry stations have ATMs. Most are linked to international networks, the most common being Cirrus, Plus, Star and Maestro.

➜ Most ATMs also spit out cash if you use a major credit card. This method tends to be more expensive because, in addition to a service fee, you'll be charged interest immediately (in other words, there's no interest-free period as with purchases). For exact fees, check with your own bank or credit card company.

➜ Visitors heading to Canada's truly remote regions won't find an abundance of ATMs, so it is wise to cash up beforehand.

➜ Scotiabank, common throughout Canada, is part of the Global ATM Alliance. If your home bank is a member, fees may be less if you withdraw from Scotiabank ATMs.

Cash

Most Canadians don't carry large amounts of cash for everyday use, relying instead on credit and debit cards. Still, carrying some cash, say $100 or less, comes in handy when making small purchases. In some cases, cash is necessary to pay for rural B&Bs and shuttle vans; inquire in advance to avoid surprises. Shops and businesses rarely accept personal checks.

Credit Cards

Major credit cards such as MasterCard, Visa and American Express are widely accepted in Canada, except in remote, rural communities, where cash is king. You'll find it difficult or impossible to rent a car, book a room or order tickets over the phone without having a piece of plastic. Note that some credit card companies charge a 'transaction fee' (around 3% of whatever you purchased); check with your provider to avoid surprises. If you are given an option to pay in your home currency, it is usually better to not accept, as they charge a higher interest rate for the point-of-sale transaction.

For lost or stolen cards, these numbers operate 24 hours:

American Express (☑800-869-3016; www.americanexpress.com)

MasterCard (☑800-307-7309; www.mastercard.com)

Visa (☑416-367-8472; www.visa.com)

Tipping

Tipping is a standard practice. Generally you can expect to tip for the following:

Restaurant waitstaff 15% to 20%

Bar staff $1 per drink

Hotel bellhop $1 to $2 per bag

Hotel room cleaners From $2 per day (depending on room size and messiness)

Taxis 10% to 15%

OPENING HOURS

Opening hours vary throughout the year. We've provided high-season opening hours; hours will generally decrease in the shoulder and low seasons.

Banks 10am–5pm Monday to Friday; some open 9am–noon Saturday

Bars 5pm–2am daily

Clubs 9pm–2am Wednesday to Saturday

Restaurants breakfast 8–11am, lunch 11:30am–2:30pm Monday to Friday, dinner 5–9:30pm daily; some open for brunch 8am to 1pm Saturday and Sunday

Shops 10am–6pm Monday to Saturday, noon–5pm Sunday; some open to 8pm or 9pm Thursday and/or Friday

Supermarkets 9am–8pm; some open 24 hours

PUBLIC HOLIDAYS

Canada observes 10 national public holidays and more at the provincial level. Banks, schools and government offices close on these days.

SAFE TRAVEL

Canada is one of the safest countries in the world. Pickpocketing and muggings are rare, especially if you take commonsense precautions. Panhandling is common, but usually not dangerous or aggressive.

➡ Stay in your car at all times when photographing wildlife.

➡ Drink spiking is rare but solo travelers should be cautious.

➡ With the exception of cannabis, recreational drug use in Canada is illegal, including magic mushrooms, and police can stop you any time you're behind the wheel.

➡ Forest fires, though rare, are a possible threat and should be treated seriously.

TELEPHONE

Canada's phone system is extensive and landlines reach most places; however, cell service can be spotty. Truly remote areas may not have any phone service at all.

Cell Phones

➡ If you have an unlocked GSM phone, you should be able to buy a SIM card from local providers such as **Telus** (www.telus.com), **Rogers** (www.rogers.com) or **Bell** (www.bell.ca). Bell has the best data coverage.

➡ US residents can often upgrade their domestic cell phone plan to extend to Canada. **Verizon** (www.verizonwireless.com) provides good results.

➡ Reception is poor and often nonexistent in rural areas no matter who your service provider is. Some companies' plans do not reach all parts of Canada, so check coverage maps.

➡ SIM cards that work for a set period, such seven, 14, 20 or 30 days, can be purchased online, often with United States and Canada voice, SMS and data bundled together.

Domestic & International Dialing

➡ Canadian phone numbers consist of a three-digit area code followed by a seven-digit local number. In many parts of Canada, you must dial all 10 digits preceded by 1, even if you're calling across the street. In other parts of the country, when you're calling within the same area code, you can dial the seven-digit number only, but this is slowly changing.

➡ For direct international calls, dial ☑011 + country code + area code + local phone number. The country code for Canada is 1 (the same as for the USA, although international rates still apply for all calls made between the two countries).

➡ Toll-free numbers begin with ☑800, 877, 866, 855, 844 or 833 and must be preceded by 1. Some of these numbers are good throughout Canada and the USA, others only work within Canada, and some work in just one province.

TOURIST INFORMATION

➡ The **Canadian Tourism Commission** (www.canada.travel) is loaded with general information, packages and links.

➡ All provincial tourist offices maintain comprehensive websites packed with information helpful in planning your trip. Staff also field telephone inquiries and, on request, will mail out free maps and directories about accommodations, attractions and events.

VISAS

Currently, visas are not required for citizens of 46 countries – including the Us, most EU members, the UK, Australia and New Zealand – for visits of up to six months.

Most arrivals from outside North America will need to fill out an eTA. Information on eTAs and visas can be found at www.cic.gc.ca/english/visit/visas.asp.

Visitor visas – aka Temporary Resident Visas (TRVs) – can now be applied for online at www.cic.gc.ca/english/information/applications/visa.asp. Single-entry TRVs ($100) are usually valid for a maximum stay of six months from the date of your arrival in Canada. In most cases your biometric data (such as fingerprints) will be taken. Note that you don't need a Canadian multiple-entry TRV for repeated entries into Canada from the USA, unless you have visited a third country.

A separate visa is required for all nationalities if you plan to study or work in Canada.

Visa extensions ($100) need to be filed at least one month before your current visa expires (www.canada.ca/en/immigration-refugees-citizenship/services/visit-canada/extend-stay.html).

BEHIND THE SCENES

SEND US YOUR FEEDBACK

We love to hear from travelers – your comments help make our books better. We read every word, and we guarantee that your feedback goes straight to the authors. Visit **lonelyplanet. com/contact** to submit your updates and suggestions.

Note: We may edit, reproduce and incorporate your comments in Lonely Planet products such as guidebooks, websites and digital products, so let us know if you are happy to have your name acknowledged. For a copy of our privacy policy visit **lonelyplanet.com/legal.**

ACKNOWLEDGMENTS

Climate map data adapted from Peel MC, Finlayson BL & McMahon TA (2007) 'Updated World Map of the Köppen-Geiger Climate Classification', *Hydrology and Earth System Sciences*, 11, pp1633–44.

Cover photograph: Yoho National Park, British Columbia, Canada; Feng Wei Photography/Getty Images ©

THIS BOOK

This 1st edition of *Canadian Rockies Best Road Trips* was researched and written by Ray Bartlett, Gregor Clark, John Lee, Craig McLachlan and Brendan Sainsbury. This guidebook was produced by the following:

Destination Editor Ben Buckner

Senior Product Editor Angela Tinson

Product Editor Kate Chapman

Cartographer Julie Sheridan

Book Designer Ania Bartoszek

Cover Researcher Fergal Condon

Thanks to Hannah Cartmel, Pete Cruttenden, Melanie Dankel, Bruce Evans, Sonia Kapoor

OUR STORY

A beat-up old car, a few dollars in the pocket and a sense of adventure. In 1972 that's all Tony and Maureen Wheeler needed for the trip of a lifetime – across Europe and Asia overland to Australia. It took several months, and at the end – broke but inspired – they sat at their kitchen table writing and stapling together their first travel guide, *Across Asia on the Cheap*. Within a week they'd sold 1500 copies. Lonely Planet was born.

Today, Lonely Planet has offices in the US, Ireland and China, with a network of more than 2000 contributors in every corner of the globe. We share Tony's belief that 'a great guidebook should do three things: inform, educate and amuse'.

INDEX

OUR WRITERS

RAY BARTLETT

Ray has been travel writing for nearly two decades, bringing Japan, Korea, Mexico, Tanzania, Guatemala, Indonesia, and many parts of the United States to life in rich detail for top-industry publishers, newspapers, and magazines. His acclaimed debut novel, *Sunsets of Tulum*, set in Yucatán, was a Midwest Book Review 2016 Fiction pick. Among other pursuits, he surfs regularly and is an accomplished Argentine tango dancer. He currently divides his time between homes in the USA, Japan and Mexico.

GREGOR CLARK

Gregor Clark is a US-based writer whose love of foreign languages and curiosity about what's around the next bend have taken him to dozens of countries on five continents. Chronic wanderlust has also led him to visit all 50 states and most Canadian provinces on countless road trips through his native North America. Since 2000, Gregor has regularly contributed to Lonely Planet guides, with a focus on Europe and the Americas.

JOHN LEE

Born and raised in the historic UK city of St Albans, John slowly succumbed to the lure of overseas exotica, and arrived on Canada's West Coast in 1993 to begin an MA in Political Science at the University of Victoria. Regular trips home to Britain ensued, along with stints living in Tokyo and Montréal, before he returned to British Columbia to become a full-time freelance writer in 1999. Now living in Vancouver, John specializes in travel writing and has contributed to more than 150 different publications around the world.

CRAIG MCLACHLAN

Craig has covered destinations all over the globe for Lonely Planet for two decades. Based in Queenstown, New Zealand, for half the year, he runs an outdoor activities company and a sake brewery, then moonlights overseas for the other half, leading tours and writing for Lonely Planet. Craig has completed a number of adventures in Japan and his books are available on Amazon. Check out www.craigmclachlan.com

BRENDAN SAINSBURY

Born and raised in the UK in a town that never merits a mention in any guidebook (Andover, Hampshire), Brendan spent the holidays of his youth caravanning in the English Lake District and didn't leave Blighty until he was 19. Making up for lost time, he's since squeezed 70 countries into a sometimes precarious existence as a writer and professional vagabond. He has written over 40 books for Lonely Planet from Castro's Cuba to the canyons of Peru.

Published by Lonely Planet Global Limited
CRN 554153
1st edition – Oct 2022
ISBN 978 1 83869 568 2
© Lonely Planet 2022   Photographs © as indicated 2022
10 9 8 7 6 5 4 3 2
Printed in China

Although the authors and Lonely Planet have taken all reasonable care in preparing this book, we make no warranty about the accuracy or completeness of its content and, to the maximum extent permitted, disclaim all liability arising from its use.